PALM ISLAND--PARADISE LOST

A STORY OF LIES, BETRAYAL, SUFFERING, AND HEALING

by
TEDDY TARR, PSY. D.

Bloomington, IN  Milton Keynes, UK

authorHOUSE®

AuthorHouse™
1663 Liberty Drive, Suite 200
Bloomington, IN 47403
www.authorhouse.com
Phone: 1-800-839-8640

AuthorHouse™ UK Ltd.
500 Avebury Boulevard
Central Milton Keynes, MK9 2BE
www.authorhouse.co.uk
Phone: 08001974150

First published by AuthorHouse 7/17/2006

ISBN: 1-4259-4771-9 (sc)

Library of Congress Control Number: 2006905814

Printed in the United States of America
Bloomington, Indiana

This book is printed on acid-free paper.

TABLE OF CONTENTS

LOVE

This attitude—that nothing is easier than to love—has continued to be the prevalent idea about love in spite of the overwhelming evidence to the contrary. There is hardly an activity, any enterprise, which is started with such tremendous hopes and expectations, and yet, which fails so regularly, as love. If this were the case with any other activity, people would be eager to know the reasons for the failure, and to learn how one could do better—or they would give up the activity. Since the latter is impossible in the case of love, there seems to be only one adequate way to overcome the failure of love—to examine the reasons for . . .failure, and to proceed to study the meaning of love.

- Erich Fromm (1956, p. 4-5, in Masterson,

Search for the Real Self)

ACKNOWLEDGEMENTS

I am grateful for family and friends who believed in my ability to complete a painful journey in a positive, creative fashion. What I learned about loss and healing evolved from years of working with my clients and from teachers.

I wish to acknowledge Dr. Noelle Stern, my editor, whose heart, commitment, creativity and unrelenting motivation for excellence propelled me chapter by chapter. Georgette and Rich have utilized their talents and enthusiasm to produce workshop materials based upon my book. They produced and printed the materials at the Copy Center right next door!

Without all the self help materials that have sustained my spirit along this pathway, I might have succumbed to the revolving door of anger and resentment. Books have entertained and enlightened by being my entire life span. I thank all the authors whose works I have quoted and have helped heal me on my journey.

My book bears testimony that within each of us lays the ability to provide lessons of healing from profound suffering we neither asked for nor deserved. I thank my clients and workshop participants who have taught me so much.

Our innate desire to isolate ourselves in moments of distress can be overcome by engaging in creative endeavors of writing and sharing our stories. This is at the heart and soul of Palm Island, Paradise Lost....... believing we can create new dreams and respond to many callings in spite of our losses. I thank everyone who has lived richly and fully following death and divorce.

And lastly I thank you, the reader with so many books to choose from – you honored mine!

IN MEMORY

In memory of my good friend, Marvin, who witnessed my tremendous struggle to survive the pain of abandonment. He offered his empathy and encouragement without question or reservation. His untimely death on April 4, 2001, was an inspiration for my journaling that marked a journey of waterfalls of tears and, finally, healing. He would have bought this book joyfully if it came with a cup of coffee and my homemade chocolate chip cookies.

FOREWORD

My whole life has been about taking responsibility for everyone and everything that came into my life and path. I grew up thinking hyper-giving would ensure success across the board, no matter what. My own inadequacies and deficiencies were protected until I was challenged to change. And my challenge, although gossips easily shrug and dismiss it in a sentence—"He wanted a divorce"—was nevertheless monumental, shaking the foundations of my life, my self, and my very physical and emotional survival.

Attempting to blend love, sex, and marriage into a committed long-term relationship is more than a challenge for a majority of our population. It is a death sentence! Individual growth has pulled out ahead of long-held values and makes for heartbreak for those who are victimized by a changing society.

In _Challenge of the Heart_, John Weldwood (1985) observes that our society produces "warriors of the heart". A sign of the times is the ability to approach the challenges of intimacy in this era of terrifying uncertainty with bravery, gentleness and, above all, a willingness to open to love's teachings by risking, and perhaps falling in love, again and again.

My heart sustained a near fatal injury and could have become hardened to betrayal by a man I thought incapable of leaving and whom I thought treasured as I did what we had together. Even a safe harbor may become stagnant for the other and silence may protect the dissolution of a relationship.

My husband was all I ever wanted or needed in a mate. Whatever tradeoffs were made in the relationship worked to my support, nurturing, and contentment.

Palm Island is the story of my survival after he left in a most abrupt and piercing way. I realized my self-deception, "that all was well" contributed to a denial of reality. His leaving forced me into self-examination, which in turn freed me from long-term anger and resentments that would have stolen the rest of my life. In the worst of times I was able to release myself from a dreaded sense of separation-anxiety that he would someday die (or I would), and I might be left in an incredibly painful state. Fears that had cocooned themselves in childhood resurfaced and impacted my ability to heal in spite of a strong sense of self, a trunk full of coping strategies, and loving, supportive family and friends.

Throughout my life, I experienced many losses and these probably helped me choose to enter the field of psychology, specializing in bereavement, sexual abuse, and divorce. I saw many couples who allowed problems to distance intimacy. I would go home at night so grateful for my husband, whom I adored. When my personal world was shattered, I was challenged to heal myself, as well as maintain a thriving practice. This is my personal story. The fact of this book is a powerful testimony to the healing I was able to produce, and I offer it to readers who are suffering as a guide on their own painful roads.

Palm Island: Paradise Lost is a collection of my notes and healing journey. I had put together a bereavement model from the literature years ago. I found it a constructive way to teach workshops and work with my private practice at Crossroads Counseling Center. I always had the most difficult time just surviving the hit that appeared out of nowhere. Using the first letter of SELF-Survival for me was the greatest challenge. I just wanted to take to my bed and pull the covers over my head.

The E in SELF is for examining. When I had managed to stabilize my emotions, I would employ my abilities to tease apart the situation, make sense of it, and try to move forward. The L in SELF represents the letting go of resentments and giving grace, totally undeserved, but necessary to move on without anger and hostility. Finally, the F in SELF – fashioning my life. This processing through the four phases of surviving, examining, letting go, and fashioning has worked for me. I skip back and forth not always in linear fashion. Additionally, I have added inner and outer circles that represent other processes that also move sort of like an old spinner game with a needle in the center. Part III p. 181-184 goes into more detail. I have included assessment sheets (Appendix A), exercises that I did (Appendix B), and helpful thoughts (Appendix C).

I came to recognize myself as the biggest threat to my sense of security and self-assurance. This was a most difficult learning laboratory. It was painful at times to record my thoughts and feelings and admit how vulnerable I was and still find myself to be. I healed my heartbreak. If you can identify yourself in my story, then perhaps you, too, can choose another pathway and other callings.

Palm Island's organizational structure follows my therapeutic bereavement/loss model. The first four chapters represent my most reactive state of being: I was like a projectile shot into a pool. I knew the mandate was swim or drown.

Chapter I – The Hit

Chapter 2 – The Hurt

Chapter 3 – The Heart

Chapter 4 – The Help

This was by far the most challenging place in which to find myself for there was no anticipatory warning. The suddenness resulted in a paralysis of thought and action that most traumatic experiences trigger. By the end of the first four months, I had formulated a plan to stabilize my life and somehow pounded in a tap root to anchor my wounded self. At times it felt like I was hanging on to a toothpick.

Chapter 5 - Examining was a recording of much writing and completing my own assessment sheets so I could keep a pulse on what I was thinking and feeling. I took copious notes. I knew from the beginning I was going to record my journey and develop workshops for others to contemplate their own healing.

Chapter 6 is a do-it-yourself journal/scrapbook project. I never liked journaling and always skipped over the exercises. My painful state was so enormous; I wrote copious outlines, poems, and articles. I think my journaling was a vehicle for my depth of understanding. I wrote my eulogy in 1988 many times and made no changes. By documenting my journey, it was as if I was co-journeying with myself. My brain and my heart were better connected than they had ever been. I referred to them as the dynamic duo.

Chapter 7 – Letting go, was a necessary part of offering grace and forgiveness for myself, my husband, and his new love. It took self-reflection, owning my own imperfections, and being willing to establish new goals. Sounds good.....took intentions, prayer, a plan, and great effort.

The tasks of Chapter 8 have been just as challenging: to reinvest in others and chance future abandonment and rejection. I might still be closely awaiting my physical death had my happiness candle stopped flickering.

Chapter 9 reflects on this Miamian saga thinking she's in recovery from an ugly betrayal, jumping into the Gulf of Mexico to heal her wounds. It was much more than the 3 ½ hour trek to go from point A to point B, as you will soon see.

The heart of Palm Island is the incredible ability of the human spirit to not only survive, but thrive in the most traumatic experiences. Come with me now as I share my heartbreak, heartache, and my painful march to embrace love fully without the fear of loss. I know now I have nothing to gain by remaining a victim. Future losses are a certainty. Future gains will happen only if I choose to reinvest in new journeys and surrender potential present and future misery. I'm up for the co-journey; we can travel together.

INTRODUCTION

THE JOURNEY OF THIS BOOK

*P*alm Island: *Paradise Lost* is a collection of my notes and journey from the shock of betrayal and divorce through a long dark night to eventual healing. In my private practice as a therapist, specializing (ironically) in bereavement, many years ago I had developed a bereavement model from the literature. I found it a constructive way to teach workshops and work with my clients at the Crossroads Counseling Center. This is the SELF model: S survival, E examining, L letting go, and F fashioning one's life. This model encourages each of us to engage in the personal work that leads to lifelong learning and growing.

Initially, Surviving (S) can be accomplished by gathering family and friends for support. Perhaps all you can do is continue to experience the pain and re-stabilize your home or move to a safe place. Legal and therapeutic help may be advisable early on to avoid making costly mistakes. Examining (E) what is happening and taking lessons from the past helps us grow. Letting Go (L) is about working through the suffering and pain and eventually offering forgiveness to ourselves and others. Fashioning (F) involves making a new pathway based on our regained strength, wisdom, and new learning. This Surviving, Examining, Letting Go, and Fashioning become a processing model for the self to follow forever. We observe our lives through the kaleidoscope of new learning and discovering.

And now, here I was, never imagining I'd be in this position, using the model myself. My greatest difficulty was simply surviving "the hit" that appeared out of nowhere. Survival for me was the greatest challenge. I just wanted to take to my bed and pull the covers over my head.

As I began to employ the E in SELF, "Examining", I managed to stabilize my emotions. Then I employed my abilities to tease apart the situation, make sense of it, and try to move forward. The L "Letting go", was hard. I had to let go of resentments and see the "offender," in this case my husband, as worthy of grace, totally undeserved, but necessary to give so I could move on without anger and hostility. Finally, as I confronted the F, "Fashioning" my life, I began to rebuild, making sense out of my life—a new life. This processing through these four phases, Surviving, Examining, Letting go, and Fashioning, has worked for me, and I share it with you. As painful as my journey has been, certainly to live and then to write about, I present it as a model for you.

I came to recognize myself as the biggest threat to my sense of security and self-assurance. This was a most difficult learning laboratory, painful to record my thoughts and feelings and admit how vulnerable I was and still find myself to be, but, through working on myself and writing, I did heal my heartbreak. If you can identify with my story, even though your details may differ, then perhaps you, too, can heal and choose another pathway and other callings.

Palm Island's structure follows this therapeutic bereavement/loss SELF model, organized according to each aspect of the model, although not always in linear fashion. Part I, Surviving, encompassing the first four chapters, and represents my most reactive state of being: Chapter 1, The Hit; Chapter 2, The Hurt; Chapter 3, The Heart; Chapter 4, The Help. I was like a projectile shot into a pool. I knew the mandate was swim or drown. This was by far the most challenging place to find myself in, for there was no anticipatory warning. The suddenness resulted in a paralysis of thought and action that most traumatic experiences trigger.

But by the end of the first four months, I had formulated a plan to stabilize my life and somehow pounded in a taproot to anchor my wounded self. Thus begins Part II, Striving, and the other facets of the "SELF" model.

Chapter 5, Examining, records much writing and completion of my own assessment sheets so I could keep a pulse on what I was thinking and feeling. Although, I never liked journaling and always skipped over the exercises to journal in books and workshops. I took copious notes on myself and my daily new awareness. I knew from the beginning—and this is part of what kept me going—that I was going to record my journey and develop workshops for others to contemplate their own healing.

Chapter 6, Documenting, is a do-it-yourself journal/scrapbook project. Despite my aversion to journaling, my painful state was so enormous that I found relief only in writing copious outlines, poems, and articles. I think my journaling was a vehicle for my depth of understanding. By documenting my journey, it was as if I was co-journeying with myself. Paradoxically, despite my writhing pain, my brain and my heart were better connected than they had ever been.

Chapter 7 – Letting Go, shows the necessary part of offering grace and forgiveness to myself, my husband, and his new love. To let go took self-reflection, owning my own imperfections, and being willing to establish new goals.

The tasks of Chapter 8, Fashioning, have been just as challenging: to recreate my life, reach out, and reinvest in others, thereby chancing future abandonment and rejection.

Part III, Thriving, reports on my healing and ever-new awareness. Chapter 9 reflects on my saga, both emotional and physical, with rituals I felt bound to enact at the actual Palm Island. It was much more than the 4½ hour trek from Miami to Palm Island to get to the shores of renewal. Chapter 10 offers an Epilogue, tying together all I have learned.

Throughout, interwoven with my own story, are thoughts and reflections from my psychological studies and practice. They helped me immeasurably in understanding and dealing with what I was going through. The Bibliography lists all those I refer to or quote. I have included tools and coping strategies from my personal experience and practice in Part I and Part II.

To help you further, I have also included assessment sheets (Appendix A), exercises I did (Appendix B), and additional helpful and inspiring thoughts (Appendix C). Of course, use the book any way you find most helpful, but I would recommend completing the assessments in Appendix A and setting up a computer file or scrapbook for yourself. As you do, this book will become more personal and meaningful.

The heart of Palm Island, and what I want to show, is the incredible ability of the human spirit to not only survive, but thrive in the most traumatic experiences. I have interwoven my own experiences and feelings with the tremendous learning from other helping professionals and constant self-examination. Hopefully, you will identify with my feelings, even if your own situation is not exactly the same. And hopefully again, you will learn from what is shared here.

Once again, I invite you to come with me as I share my heartbreak, heartache, and my painful march to re-embrace love fully without the fear of loss. I know I have nothing to gain by remaining a victim. Future losses are a certainty. Future gains will take place only if I choose to reinvest in new journeys and surrender present and imagined future misery. I have taken the journey. Take my hand, share my heart, we can travel together.

PART I – SURVIVING

Agent: The Inactive, Reactive Me

SURVIVING

Introduction

Our first instinct is to survive. In a traumatic loss, we keep returning to the survival period until we can move from reactive to taking action. Chapter 1, The Hit, is a personal narrative reflecting on a life that was idyllic, poisoned by first a cheating spouse, and later victimized by my perfectionist self. Since my bereavement-centered practice involves a working through process, so does uncoupling. So, Chapters 1-4 comprise the survival phase of the SELF model, characterized by intense emotional reactions, especially fear, anger, and sadness. Surviving includes surviving "The Hit" (Chapter. 1), "The Hurt" (Chapter 2), "The Heartbreak" (Chapter 3), and "The Help" (Chapter 4).

This book conceptualizes the process as a journey undertaken by pilgrims seeking healing and new direction. It takes courage to embark on a personal journey when you feel so disheartened. Despite my resistance and obstacles, I learned I could not only survive but thrive. More in the chapters ahead...come with me and trust yourself to take what you need for your own unique self, from Palm Island.

CHAPTER 1

"THE HIT"

The Bomb Drops

My husband and I boarded the ferry for a five-minute ride across the channel to Palm Island, off the west coast of Florida, near Port Charlotte. I had lived in Miami for the past thirty years but never felt as at home as here, and came here every chance I could. Talcum-powdered beaches border the Gulf of Mexico while a parade of vessels scurries back and forth on the Intracoastal Waterway. There is little commercialism, and the natural beauty seems to have tamed even developers' greed. I loved fishing off the dock and soaking up the island beauty like a sponge. I not only fell in love with the island, but I was enraptured with my imagined simple lifestyle. It was the perfect place to write, and I fantasized how I could author the book I had secretly been developing for the past two years on bereavement.

When we landed—a too-short transition from the city—my husband's friends greeted us warmly as we invaded their three-story home overlooking the waterway.

I must admit my husband was not smitten by the beauty of Palm Island, or the island culture. He seemed unimpressed and commented on how remote and isolated he felt. Apparently, he experienced the primitive haven as inconvenient for practical purposes. I was shocked when he once asked, "Do you really think you would be happy here?"

At my suggestion several years ago, he not only bought a lot, but contracted also for a dock. But my enthusiasm was dampened somewhat when he announced we could retire elsewhere and use our Palm Island place as an investment. Nevertheless, I could hardly contain my excitement after our purchase.

I ordered blueprints from a coastal magazine, began pouring over the plans, and immersed myself in the latest building materials. I pictured all our family and friends delighting in our new retreat. I loved my dream, but knew, also, in the rational part of my mind, that it was kind of silly. I've always lived in the here and now, and retirement was a long eight to ten years away.

On a muggy Sunday evening in August of 2000, we had just returned from Palm Island. It had been a wonderful weekend, with our simpatico friends, walking on the beach, giggling over the spitting giant pots of water cooking the fresh shellfish, and snuggling on the sofa after a huge dinner with carafes of coffee. Once home, our bags thrown in a corner of the bedroom to be dealt with later, my husband sat down heavily on the lounge chair and mumbled in a soft depressive voice, "I have something to tell you that you are not going to want to hear."

I felt my throat tighten, and numbness spread throughout my body. The Friday before we left he had completed an executive physical, and I braced myself for what I thought would be a disastrous report. I sat down close by on the bed.

He spit it out--"You have three days to gather your clothes and move out. I have fallen in love with a former love. Take everything you own. She will eventually be moving in, and at some point, we will be married. This is not up for discussion. I want a divorce. There is nothing more to say."

No words can express my inner torment!

Every abandonment feeling or thought competed for my attention on a cellular level. I was in shock. No call to 911 could save me. Later, I would journal this favorite passage from a work entitled, "Resurrection" by L.C.M. (This is a poem put out with these initials. I don't remember where I obtained it.)

> For my fingers could not grip and
> I slipped in the sand, moaning, crying
> in the howling wind, crawling to a
> corner to await my own destruction,
> caring no longer for myself, my world,
> those within.

I called in a spiritual prayer circle and asked for divine intervention. Suzanne Kardatzke, a close friend, came to my aid. I accused God of wanting more of my attention than I could surrender. In my wildest most self-tormenting dreams, my husband was the last person in the world whom I would have distrusted. And, he not only betrayed me, he lied in the process: she wasn't a former love, but a current coworker.

It was my worst nightmare! But he left no choice; his ultimatum was clear.

The next day I began packing my clothes, throwing out a lot of things in a quiet rage that I could hardly identify, and moved to a temporary tiny apartment.

Two days later, he called from work and said, "Stop moving! I've changed my mind. We'll talk later."

I returned, tiptoeing around the house, terrified that my very breathing might send him into her arms. But lies, betrayal, and manipulation would surface over the next few months. I discovered that he had inadvertently mailed a Victoria's Secret receipt to me for **her** Christmas present. It was accidentally tucked into some other papers. It really hurt. My faith was severely tested. I had entered a desert with no anticipatory warning. My mind wanted to make sense of it, while my heart remained out of touch with reality, flooded with feelings that drowned all reason.

I was willing to forgive him of anything to avoid the pain. We went on a vacation to Niagara Falls, which proved a disaster. He was as cold and distant as the icy water.

On January 25, 2001, five months later, he made another announcement. It was over, he said. He had never ended the relationship with her and wanted to end our marriage.

From the time I'd moved back, I'd had an uneasy awareness that he was in a quandary, even though we resumed what appeared to be a normal life and I kept clinging to his superficially hopeful words, "I've changed my mind", so I had not unpacked.

Physically, it was somewhat less chaotic than the first time. I was ruthless with paring down my possessions, giving to Goodwill treasures of long ago. I took only essentials and nothing of my husband's.

But emotionally, I was devastated. My heart was empty, out of hope, for a future resolution, rather than dissolution. He'd never, I realized, really wanted to talk about anything, but had used that "extension," in which I dared to believe we would reconcile, as a testing ground. And it worked for him, confirming his first chilling pronouncement.

I tried reasoning with him through a cascade of tears. How could this be happening to a thirty-year friendship, the last twelve of which were a coupleship? I thought I was losing my mind! I knew he had lost his! I had begged, pleaded, and cried while he maintained his newly manifested indifference. I thought I was negotiating with an alien.

He said he wanted to be with someone he loved as much as I loved him. Could it really be that simple?

Reluctantly, I moved out. Legally, I knew I could have dragged my feet, but, against all rational signals, I was still too hopeful not to obey, and I was being forced into a move I didn't want. I couldn't allow myself to think it was over, because I still loved my husband. But this is like thinking you have money in a barren bank account because you have checks.

He had changed his mind once, and I figured I would wait it out. But it didn't take long for him to serve me with divorce papers. So much for my ability to second- guess anything.

All I believed in and had lived was being questioned. How could I have missed this? We'd always seemed close. How could our relationship be so wonderful for me and so terrible for him? I knew I would probably never have the answers.

Sex had never been important to him . . . not even in the most passionate of times. I was more emotional, sensual, and sexual. He was considerate, loving, and giving in a different way. I curbed myself from calling him often at work, although I always wanted to, just to hear his voice, just to have reassurance. And, he often called me.

He'd always set the tone of the relationship, and we had a nice routine. I cooked five nights a week and he picked up takeout twice a week. On Saturday mornings, after breakfast out, we shopped together. We had friends we both enjoyed, watched many sports events on TV together (with him in charge of the remote), and observed all holidays with my four grown children, with a banquet I always prepared enthusiastically and creatively. My husband was the beloved, over-idealized, and the author of the past twelve years of Camelot. I felt the "penance" I'd undergone from three bad marriages had finally paid off.

But I would never really understand, because now I saw there had been no real communication. I had been totally happy, and he was plodding through, suffering

6

in silence. The "Why"? question rarely gets satisfaction. I was microscopically over-analyzing, and trying to blame myself, when he was clearly stating he was leaving me for someone else. I'm sure he refused to say more because I was in rigor mortis.

I had kept my home prior to my marriage. Unfortunately, it was only ten minutes away. It was unnerving to think of seeing him driving his car nearby. I avoided all accidental encounters. My first concern was for my mental health—how best could I take care of myself? It takes two to make a relationship, but only one to break it. I knew I needed to construct an emergency plan . . . simple, flexible, and the least stressful possible.

My second concern was for my practice. After all, I was a psychologist and had an active bereavement practice. Clients, who were hurting mightily, were counting on me, and I needed to set a framework to protect them. And, I was a busy workshop leader, with many dates I had to fulfill. It was essential I maintain my equilibrium.

There were more unanswered questions than answers. I felt the pain and sorrow were engulfing, but I refused to do anything I would later regret with previous losses, and as I advised my clients with serious professionalism, I had learned my best ploy was to focus first on healing myself before blowing away a significant relationship. I needed all of myself to survive "The Hit".

My husband attempted to obtain my signature to sell the Palm Island property, which he had placed in both our names. First, he said he would never want to live there. I offered to sign it over if he would put this in writing. He then said he might build a home there—for *her*. Lied again. Just when I thought it couldn't get worse, the elevator fell another fifty feet with no ground in sight. Despite my terrible emotional turmoil, I refused to sign away my already shattered dream.

Initially, I felt like someone had died . . . ME! I was traumatized and in total disbelief, refusing to accept my reality. It was much like I had felt when family or friends had died.

His indifference to my suffering was unbelievable! I obviously was not getting it, in part because he pretended to offer a relationship of hope. He had inferred he was undecided, inviting me back, to lower my hurt and manipulate my love for the impending divorce for which he longed. Just as he always controlled the TV remote, he was trying to control our divorce. He pleaded with me to use a friend of his as my attorney. I was at least able to see through this—a friend of his! So my husband would have a direct pipeline to my legal dealings? No, thank you. I refused to engage in anything legal until I had consulted someone—certainly not a friend of his—whom I knew was going to represent my best interests.

It was all I could do to find a safe emotional and mental place to deal with my helplessness, hopelessness, and haplessness. I was so ashamed this was happening to me. I felt my personal life was over!

I lost my husband in the most humiliating way of all—to another woman.

I lost my friends.

I lost Palm Island and my dream.

I felt like I had lost myself!

I practiced my art as a psychologist and seminar leader, compartmentalizing and shielding my professional life from my personal one. Against all evidence, I was still ridiculously hopeful the relationship would magically return to what I thought I'd had. My heart was unwilling to surrender to the truth. Secretly and privately, even with the accelerating march of the divorce, I waited for word that he had again changed his mind. That word never came.

Rumination and Enervation

I never saw it coming! It drove me absolutely crazy, as his wife, (not to mention being a psychologist) that I could be ambushed, betrayed, rejected, and cast out in less than three minutes. His words that dreadful August night haunted me for months and years. How ironic my life was: At the time, I was giving spiritual workshops and lecturing on the Biblical Book of Job.

I was feeling more like the main character than the workshop facilitator, unable to make sense of any or all of it.

Initially, I collected myself, calling my four adult children and two close friends, and poured out my grief. They rallied to my aid, two of them taking flights from New York, and devoted themselves to me. We cried together. They had all been close with my husband, and it was a loss for all of us.

I called my prayer circle in Indianapolis, led by an accomplished Prayer Warrior, who prayed for a reunion. No one believed he would walk away, and everyone tried to convince me it wasn't over.

I felt God was sending me a message. The timing of my husband's decision to end the marriage and my six Job workshops were more than coincidental. Was God saying: "It is over; your suffering is beginning and, by the way, listen to Job". I had to conclude there is no untouchable, inviolate, invulnerable relationship.

It was such an enigma--the marriage had seemed so vital. The only choice was to accept the meaningless act of aggression and surprise as beyond my comprehension. I was spinning--caught up in a downward spiral of separation–and served with divorce papers. There was no respite. I writhed with the irony: How many times had I listened to other men and women tell their tales of woe?

Others had related experiences of separation after ten or twenty years of marriage with similar shocking circumstances and this ambush-like outcome. I knew unprovoked divorce had come of age. No longer does the dictum "married or buried" hold a candle to the dissolution of a relationship for trading up to something perceived as better.

Of course, one partner leaving the marriage for an affair is neither a novel nor dramatic plot. It's the stuff of women's movies and scandalous supermarket articles. What is incredible is the cloak-and-dagger betrayal that takes place right smack in the middle of a marriage that by all appearances is solid and satisfying.

In the first few months of the disaster, my life felt frozen in time, like eons-old stone, incapable of movement. I was terrified of facing a single lifestyle in the future, and felt paralyzed, almost physically, and certainly in all my motivational components. I forced myself to settle into new surroundings. After a while, exhaustion at denial too much, I stopped fighting it, made peace with the pain, and rested the few times I could. Slowly the paralysis subsided.

I felt exhausted. It was an exhausting time. The only positive I saw was that at least I wasn't responsible for young children. I knew this state of mourning very well—from my own many losses, and certainly living through my clients' losses. Yes, I was a pro. As the paralysis faded, in its place came full-blown mourning and a loss of my joy. I had been a joyous person most of the time, paradoxically despite my profession and the enormous suffering I saw daily. But I loved my practice, I loved my office, I loved my seminars, I loved my home life, and I loved my husband.

But now—I knew only what seemed like an eternal joyless state. My lifeboat was on the river of mediation/divorce. What a voyage! Like a home made raft in the midst of a typhoon. I never knew if I'd make it to land, much less through the next engulfing wave.

I knew from my voluminous readings, for my doctorate and beyond, that in this early survival state, we alternate between trying to avoid our situation and re-experiencing it. We go through both types of experiences intellectually, emotionally, behaviorally, physiologically, and spiritually. It is a natural human response to sudden negative, uncontrollable events to first find ourselves in shock and disbelief.

Our cognitive and behavioral responses involve a mourning process of working through loss for the threat/death of a desired relationship. We become preoccupied with the situation, full of guilt and shame, and exhibit physical symptoms of anxiety, sleeplessness, and appetite disturbances, forcing food down or gorging on all the wrong things. And we commonly lose all interest in formerly pleasurable things.

And now, all my readings, note-taking, and previous experiences came home. I felt like a receptacle of all the books come to life, all the case studies rising up like the undead and putting their curses on me, all the clients howling in my ears and brain at once. And the pain was constantly worse because of the supreme irony—the professional dealt the same blow as her clients. I don't know which was worse, the pain of losing him or the humiliation that I hadn't seen it coming.

Studies vary on the recovery time following a loss. However, many struggle two to four years trying to reestablish a new lifestyle. There is a need to identify all that has been lost and a need to recognize anew who one is, where one is, and begin to fashion new goals. First, you need to travel the legal pathway to protect what is legally yours. It is quite a disadvantage to love a person who is dismissing you like a bad office temp and offering you a termination package that looks like a corporate takeover. He had suggested mediation and I agreed.

Let's Make a Deal

Mediation is an attempt to avoid court costs and have disputing parties come to an equitable settlement. Nevertheless, it is still an expensive proposition and there is no guarantee there will be an amicable division of goods, let alone shared parental guidelines or any other gray-area issue. Neither mediation nor divorce is set in moral arenas. The legal system may render a decision that is neither morally nor legally fair. Division may impact both individuals, family members, and all future relationships, either positively or negatively. Whichever side engages the best attorney and has the necessary staying power certainly operates from an advantage and position of influence.

Unlike Monopoly, the one with more money is not guaranteed continued building of hotels and enjoyment of a higher standard of living. Money never erases the suffering, shame, or humiliation for either partner. However, without adequate financial resources, one battles to meet the lowest level of physical needs: food, clothing, and shelter. How was I to restore myself?

For me, the mediation was more like pacification. Let me explain. Around the campfire gathered the mediator, an attorney, my husband's attorney and assistant, my attorney and assistant, some strange attorney observer, whose presence was never explained, and the "neutral" accountant. Oh, yes, and the psychologist—me of course, we met in my husband's attorney's conference room. There was no discussion or debate about that—just like he controlled the TV remote.

The accountant announced immediately how wonderfully detailed all of my husband's records were. (He had long been this way, which I could label in psycho-speak as anal-retentive, obsessive-compulsive, and a host of other terms that also boiled down to his insatiable drive to control.) All the estimates of the antiques were Macy's bargains. So all my years of collecting were, in a few moments, down the drain.

For everyone else, it is a split of dollars. But with the antiques, I was splitting my vacation treasures financially, and of course taking none of them, losing everything I loved! None of the others present cared one iota! He had my 6-year-old car and all the jewelry he had purchased for me itemized on narrow-lined ultra-neat sheets. You think a psychologist keeps a list of business suits, is reimbursed

11

for her painting and wall papering the home, or logs in countless hours of raking leaves?

Sorry, I thought our lives were melded together. For him, it must have been like two flasks of oil and water that look like one until you see the glass wall. Not a bad metaphor--I felt like a salad, tossed about uncontrollably by him and his entourage, unable to separate myself from my marriage.

To add insult to injury, my own attorney never once got my name right. He called me "Terry" the entire day. To say anything would have added more insult to all the ambulance-worthy injuries. What I thought was to be a stable financial package became a nightmare. I know he gave me what my husband felt I was worth, now that I was no longer his partner. I couldn't recover the last ten years; a broken heart has no price tag. With all the touted pluses of mediation, there is no such thing as a "good divorce" if you don't want one! Without representation, I would have given away the farm and probably gone with it as hired help. At least my attorney, although inattentive to my name, did look out for my finances.

So, our lives divided like the Red Sea. I survived the mediation and shamefully slithered away. Only once, 2 years later, did we run into each other near my office. I said hello and called him by name. He stared for a moment, and said the unthinkable written across his face, "I didn't recognize you." He embarrassed himself and clearly was uncomfortable. Half-jokingly I replied, "Perhaps that was part of the problem in the marriage." Just knowing he was five minutes away from my office weighed heavily on my heart. My love was not turned off.

It would be nice if divorce could wrap up into a neat little package and all the thoughts and feelings be thrown away. But they continue to travel for years from the initial hit to both the past and the future. My writing reflects the incredible need to make sense of the marriage as much as the divorce. Everything triggered everything. I had to quiet myself and remind myself constantly that this too would pass.

Survival is not an end goal. It is a reactive state where one tries to constrict one's world to deal with a traumatic experience. The life I had with my husband ended when he made it very clear it was over. I knew I needed to examine our relationship and figure out how I managed to miss so many clues to what was going on. My husband was the last person on the planet I would have believed unfaithful. His cruelty was unfathomable.

My life was being fashioned, but not yet by me. Everything in the beginning was reactive and over-reactive. I was flooding my very core with self-loathing for being so blind. I soothed myself whenever I could, but I couldn't stop the poisoned arrows that seemed to come from nowhere, directed at my being. I was convinced my husband was trying to destroy me; only later would I take responsibility for the narcissistic wounding by my own hands. I waited until I was able to function on a higher level before doing anything really cerebral. I journaled what was going on and wrote the first part of this chapter. Letting go was not a possibility concerning either the pain or anger I was experiencing. I knew this was mandatory to free myself for other creative endeavors. I had never learned how to shut off the suffering faucet.

Early Losses/Later Crosses

In therapy, both partners have to let go in different ways. The relationship is not really ended by divorce or death. Feelings have to be worked through as the ties are broken. Unprocessed feelings will inevitably surface and intensify abandonment, rejection, and anger. By working through earlier traumatic experiences, I released some painful places long repressed. My heavy heart was attempting to disentangle twelve years' worth of a committed, invested relationship and thirty years of friendship. It seemed like such an impossible task, and I felt absolutely destroyed. I had so much to do, including physical relocation, not to mention mental and emotional restructuring. Where do I begin?

The abandonment issues in the present were being triggered by the past, adding to my devastation. I was emotionally drained and reacted in maximum ways, increasing my suffering. My personal resources and support team were gratefully in place, but I postponed/refused to take self-control. To tell the truth, my heart was so broken I had great difficulty mobilizing the troops. Emotional loneliness, with its roots in infancy, set in almost immediately. Whatever the earlier remaining residue from prior losses was now triggered and became painfully present once again.

Looking back, I see I was fighting years of a possible abandonment depression. Instead of identifying my obstacles to recovery, I became the obstacle. Like an intuitive lifeline, I kept journaling, knowing I would some day want to go back in and make sense of everything. But at this point, I couldn't clarify goals or options because of my intense feelings of grief.

I was terrified of being alone and wanted to feel safe. It would be months before I could readdress my economic losses. Hurt and pain were highly visible and almost palpable from the outset, but anger cloaked itself for months. Moral outrage at times threatened to overtake me. Everything in me fought relinquishing what had been lost: my husband, my marriage, our home, my lifestyle, and Palm Island, a future idyllic retirement dream and reality. My ego had been hammered and was reeling from "the hit", and I couldn't create or accept any corrective experience and make it all okay. Pessimism and cynicism vied for my energy and almost won. They could have threatened my health.

But my core worth refused to wave a white flag and surrender to a permanent disability. Out of the wreckage would emerge a new self, a new pathway. The existential void would disappear because I had a portfolio of trauma credits. In fact, the profession has now acceded to a real diagnosis for what I was experiencing, called "Broken Hearts." It is derived from symptoms evolving from a failed relationship through death or divorce.

My personal past narrative was that of an over-comer. My choice of career was the direct result of working through and transcending multiple losses. All the uncontrollable, overwhelming events of childhood resulting in emotional flooding had disappeared. I had faced my demons, taken responsibility for my self-healing, and, for the most part, had replaced despair with repair.

I knew I had to face my fear. There would be no surrender to a robotic existence, devoid of empathy. I refused to let fear take control. Taking stock of all my options was tearful. I had no one book to go to. My faith sustained me while I wandered in search of another pathway. I had believed self-effacious people have control over their life circumstances and always tried new things. I had persisted in activities through countless setbacks. And, I had always known that adversity might delay but not abort my journey. These beliefs were resilient to total shattering, but I struggled continuously, fighting my desire to pull off and isolate myself.

But I knew too, that traumatic experiences can create a total remodeling, transformation of our feelings, thoughts, and behaviors. Profound experiences can affect our entire belief system, for good or ill. Our inner resources and resilience dictate how we will come out of trauma, crushed, or more greatly purposeful.

After the divorce, I knew my intense feelings and thoughts were probably out of proportion to what was happening. I was being flooded by all my earlier losses plus the divorce. I liked my personal story. Like a spectator in the crowd, I witnessed myself, Joan-like, being burned at the stake, while I tried throwing buckets of water on the pyre. But now, the hyper-arousal—feelings so deep and intense—were impairing my ability to see a personal future. With the competing thoughts of early abandonment re-triggered, and my intruding professional assessments, I felt as if cast into Job's whirlwind, I could hardly accept the chaos, and certainly not with his patience.

All I Never Learned in Kindergarten

When childhood is traumatically impacted by negative events, sometimes the need for order and control triggers a personality needing and showing of a high level of achievement and motivation. Self-worth and performance are somehow equated. Stress is coped with in self-defeating ways, such as ruminative thoughts, self-blame, and over-generalization of failures. As I reflect back to adolescence, I can see how my own early childhood—especially in adolescence—contained some self-sabotaging. Fears of rejection and loneliness were warded off by trying to please everyone. I would minimize my own anger, often swallowing it to maintain relationships, sometimes blaming myself. This over-idealization towards men resulted In a negative self-image when a relationship would end. Self-loathing and fault finding said more about how I was treated as a child than what was happening.

I knew my husband had over-idealized me from a distance prior to marriage. He was intolerant of small mistakes. I sought to blame myself for the rejection. By trying to please others and be perfect, I could distance the emotional wolves of childhood. From my own past, I knew I had this constellation and the attendant perfectionist tendencies. Actually, I was sort of a "recovered perfectionist," so good with my self-talk that it was less of a pragmatic problem than the way I

15

thought about myself in this one area. And, for the most part, I routinely reined them in. I more than survived. For all purposes, I looked like the picture postcard teenager—high functioning academically, social, and spiritual. It came at a great price: inner suffering that showed in relationships.

In contrast, though, I wasn't so other-oriented with high expectations for their behaviors. Nor did I think society expected more out of me than I did of myself. We are all so well defended from fully understanding our motives by being able to make excuses, accuse others, and lie to ourselves. When "the hit" occurred, it went right through my defenses and my ability to protect myself. I felt shame at the thought of being rejected, let alone at all the losses I would experience from no longer being a couple.

I had no control over the situation, and my divorce was a given—even though, in spite of all the agonizing actualities—I kept denying this. I had personal experience with prior breakups, but they paled in comparison to this. Why? I thought I had so well learned the earlier lessons. Clearly, hostility and impatience surfaced for me, as much because of my lack of personal power as being rejected. My own empowerment was thwarted by the rejection triggering all the bad feelings from childhood. In spite of all the knowledge and coping strategies, I was being submerged with fears of rejection, shame, and guilt.

This emotional security was a part of my early survival that I battled for. The inability to be totally honest in a relationship was missing. The ability to turn off intense emotions that rose from my inner emotional bone yard had served me well until now. I had not been tested over the past twelve years, feeling relatively safe in the marriage. I felt loved and cherished. I know now I was over investing in order to maintain the inner calm. This had an addictive quality.

Emotional security was a luxury and scarce in my early years. The inability to be totally honest in a loving relationship was missing. I co-created with my husband an artificial relationship where many areas were avoided. Self-deception kept the true problems and any underlying hostility from observation. Business offered a channel to cover up what was truly going on. An addiction is anything you are doing that you know is bad for you, but you keep on doing it anyway--alcohol, drugs, credit card usage, sex, food, even too much sleep. No one needs to feel you get "extra credit" for doing this alone. I certainly didn't handle my grief alone; I immediately called family and friends, who rallied around instantly.

But you still have to experience the feelings alone; no one can do it for you. Whatever it takes—the pain, shock, regret, self-recrimination, sadness, loneliness, fear, rage. I found "taking the hit"—experiencing the sadness and pain and all that went with these—paradoxically and therapeutically helped me let go of my suffering. But it was a long, painful journey. My fantasy that all was paradise, and avoidance of what surely must have been clues, certainly prolonged my agony and didn't help to rebuild positive outcomes.

When one partner leaves, he or she must consider the economics, social isolation, breaking of vows, the family constellation and new family bonds that have been forged, and all the changes that will ensue. Likely way before the final dreaded announcement, the partner has struggled with whether to stay or go. In *Splitting Up*, Pam and Pearson (1998) estimate the average time of contemplation before dissolution is four years. For the partner leaving, once disenchantment has set in solidly, a dead relationship is the only choice. Often, the other partner will try to hijack the exit, feeling overwhelmed at being abandoned. (He made sure of my silence by feeding my love addiction. He hinted he might change his mind. I would remain on hold until he wore out his extramarital affair. How sick!)

Betrayal is never felt so fully as when a partner is replaced in secrecy by someone else. Probably the person exiting has engaged in a dress rehearsal to leave many times. Sometimes the cheater will pick a fight or make false accusations. Not uncommon for one to set up a departure over time. Pam and Pearson point out that the uncoupling begins as a quiet, unilateral processing, almost unconscious or haphazard at first, hardly recognized even by the initiator. Later, accusations are made that the abandoned partner was too distant to recognize the infidelity. The double life allows the rejecter to sustain the benefits of a marriage at the same time as the freedom of being single. Eventually, the cheaters are either discovered or uncover themselves. It is no wonder that the displaced partner feels he/she is powerless to enact any change, realizing that the leaving mate has a whole new life waiting around the divorce corner.

Experiencing the Grief

The grief is not linear. It is not like you suffer the most initially and then begin getting better as time goes on. You expect to sigh with slight relief after a particularly bad night, or middle of the day. But it's not like this. Rather, the waves come over you, flood you, and then ebb back a little, giving mercy. But then, when you least expect it, there it is again—the overwhelming sadness, sorrow, tears, fears, anxiety. These feelings will ebb and flow for some time, sometimes feeling unbearable, other times almost bearable, while you work through the grief and mourning. A problem solving focus may help, but it will not necessarily take away the pain.

And what does that favorite psychological phrase "work through" mean? To me, working through a loss is to first identify what has happened. Second, to address what the losses are. (Additionally, I might note if there are any gains.) Third, I would take one issue at a time, use problem solving, coping strategies, and self-talk. Fourth, I would self-sooth any remaining areas that needed attention, having exhausted the above on each and every issue. Fifth, I would record my journey and new understanding. Sixth, I would turn to forgiveness to let go of pain and sorrow. A thirty-year friendship, a ten-year marriage, and everything I had invested emotionally crashed in a matter of minutes. As I said, it was not linear; maybe it shouldn't be. Maybe we need the re-experiencing to gradually let our defenses down and take in the horror, mold it, incorporate it into our beings, and come out, hopefully better.

But the ripples continued to drown all hopes, dreams and memories of a hoped-for future. I was too confounded, sad, and mad, to re-experience even the good times. It was like seeing your name on a blackboard one minute, and then wiped off without ceremony, replaced with another. My future stopped dead in its tracks. Sunsets were now going to be experienced alone. I was so capable of slinging insult and injury to my wounded self. The frustration of helplessness was almost unbearable. The door to my future had been closed. I kept contaminating it with fear and dread from my loss of trust in piloting my life. More than anything, I wanted to flee. Then I wanted to hide. And eventually, I knew I would have to learn how to fly again.

At one of those last scenes, like a tragic women's-channel movie, my ex-husband remarked, "Even my mother thought I should leave the marriage if I found myself unhappy." At the time, she was in an urn on the fireplace. I replied, "Have you asked lately? Maybe she has changed her mind". Not very nice of me to be sure, but after all a poor rebuttal to complete dismissal. I felt as dead as she.

Conscious love should be a work of art. And since jealousy is the dragon in paradise, my dragon disappeared with my loss of hope. Letting go ought to be permitted by law, preordained, with a magic button to release all the emotion. In *Challenges of the Heart*, Orage (p. 24) says that great love can both let go and take hold. But to let go is harder than those words indicate. We are in the end solitary! All relationships end in separation, death, or divorce.

"The hit" and accompanying hurt remind me that life is a series of separations. This one, betrayal and a divorce, is to me a threat to survival itself. I found myself having to go back inside and ponder who I am in the relationship and where I was now. How would I ever embark on a healing journey? My self-reflection was working overtime.

I needed to find, and then expose myself to, the self-examining process that would help me take the lessons forward. My vulnerability surfaced and clarity seemed so remote. What had happened to that bridge of communication we built together and the closeness I'd always experienced with him? It wasn't that he embodied the archetype of a perfect husband; he was just what I wanted, no more, no less. This was the safety place that was most polluted when the dream was shattered.

I ruminated for a long time over all the opportunities and possibilities lost when my husband departed. I continued to return to the same place each time I analyzed the relationship. Only the leftovers of my marriage remain. It would take a forensic team to understand how I could have been so disillusioned by myself! It was a perfect union except for one thing—there was no intimacy from my partner. This was the real hit—a one-sided loveless union. It was much too scary to travel there.

The hit of hits led to the truth of truths: whenever the poverty of depending on someone else is exposed, first it brings emptiness and then, finally, opens us up to the aliveness of ourselves. No one can ever really give us all we need in the way we need it or in a promissory note that it will forever be there. An asexual relationship resembles much more that of parent and child than a marital union. A perfect union appears in our visionary and romantic minds to be nearly possible but is always a remote fantasy. And this perfection probably resembles more closely that infant-mother bond and the oneness we all, inevitably, had to lose to grow into semi-dependent children and then adults.

To accept less than honesty and openness is only postponing the inevitable death of the bond. His termination notes equaled a cutting off of a major source of joy and aliveness. He would jot little things down on his stationery for me as helpful hints on how to operate my life. Or, he would ask for something. Recently, he called looking for the title to a car, accusing me of losing it. Ah ha, it was her car, not mine! How fast he back-pedaled when he realized his mistake. There was no apology. These were hurtful messages for a long time. Over and over I would need to explore the hurt and make sense of the hemorrhaging I was experiencing. Whatever mistakes I had made would have to be uncovered later. All I could do in my first endless hour of desperation was to sit in the fire and accept my painful state of affairs. The flames of rejection, betrayal, inadequacy, and humiliation burned away at me.

I've been in a survival mode before, and in time adapted to the changes and much later experienced growth. But now, what was asked of me seemed to be as difficult to accept as the pain! If I was going to reinvent myself, I better have a great set of blueprints! My identity, it felt, had vanished. Our identities are constructed in relationship to all the loved ones in our lives. A loss represents a void and an inability to continue the shared memories that are unique to that relationship.

I had worked so hard to be a good partner, or so I thought. The helplessness I felt resulted from my inability to influence the outcome of my marriage. Although I had the social support of my family and friends, they too had lost him from their circles—they had always had a great relationship with him and we'd spent many happy holidays and vacations together. So they too were angry and in mourning for my loss.

I reasoned that my feelings of isolation from this uncontrollable and overwhelming event would negatively impact anyone regardless of the level of coping skills. Probably other psychologists and professionals facing similar losses with anemic childhoods would be in despair for some time. It helped for me to normalize my own experience. I knew this was not a sign of poor recovery, but rather evidenced a strong sense of connection between my feeling states and significant relationships. Suffering is the outcome of a lost love and will not be denied. I couldn't reason or talk my way out of this one. It was going to take time and intention to tease all my losses out and let go of the overwhelming negativity from so much disappointment in myself and so many unmet goals.

I had been married and divorced before. The difference was that this relationship was working close to 95% of the time, or so I thought. First, I had married my childhood sweetheart and had four children. After the divorce, I was single for over ten years and married a man for nine months, divorced him for his immoral behavior, and lived alone for several years. I again met someone and was married five years until he took a job in Africa (he is still there ten years later). I don't like dating nor would I just live with someone. I am willing to commit and have had stable relationships of some varying duration. All my familial relationships have remained stable my entire life. I still remain friends with the father of my four children and his wife. When I married my friend after a 20-year friendship, I thought it was forever. I was not given a choice to work on the marriage. It was over before I ever knew what hit me. I still don't have all the answers as to why.

Chapter I: Reflection

"The Hit"

Pre-Flood:

"My life is like a stroll upon the beach as near the ocean's edge as I can go."

Thoreau

Post-Flood: "The Hit"

My heart took the hit. It fixated on restoring what was unobtainable: my husband's love.

My Self-Portrait

Hit with an elephant-like stun gun, I felt paralyzed. My losses were like dominos shaking back into the early childhood I had extricated myself from. A pity party ensued, only reaffirming hopelessness, helplessness, and haplessness. The devastation was engulfing. It was so apparent: It wasn't only about the rejection. I had fallen fifty floors down an elevator shaft. Sitting at the bottom was all I could do.

Lessons from Chapter 1

1. All the king's horses and all the king's men couldn't have put me together again. I would have to take responsibility for the hit of hits. I didn't want to.

2. Hope that springs eternal is often outside of reality. The fantasy was he would come to his senses. The reality was I needed to come to mine!

3. Never build a case against yourself. In the end, you have you to soothe and coax yourself into a new pathway. It was my own hands that were cutting off my air. That realization allowed me to assess what happened, what I had, what I lost, and what I could do about it. Blaming and shaming him was not only pointless and fruitless, but stealing energy I needed to redirect myself to new goals. I hated knowing this! It limited my self-pity and forced action plans…well, at least thoughts toward action plans.

Your Self-Portrait

1. Write about your "own hit" when you received the news it was over. Include doubts prior to the breakup and all the details you would like to forget.
2. Own your own part in the breakup...and no more. Was childhood full of losses? Talk about how one loss seems to trigger all losses.
3. Use the self-assessment sheets in Appendix I. You will be asked to reevaluate yourself at the close of Part IV.

Chapter 2 talks about the pain and suffering from losing a loved one.

Post-it

You may find it helpful to choose a saying from Appendix B to put on the refrigerator or make up your own.

My Chapter I Post-It

"I think I can...I think I can...I can, I can, I can."
The Little Engine that Could, Piper

(You may choose more than one.)

4. You see yourself:
   a) weak
   b) numb & in shock
   c) angry, vengeance seeking
   d) sad, lonely
   e) competent, strong

5. You feel you are:
   i) in reality
   ii) in fantasy
   iii) in denial

6. Identify three ways you can help yourself accept what has happened:

   a. _____

   b. _____

   c. _____

7. You are feeling……….. (choose any that fit.)

   ❑ Embarrassed

   ❑ Shamed

   ❑ Angry

   ❑ Guilt-ridden

   ❑ Confused

   ❑ Depressed

   ❑ Anxious

   ❑ Rejected

8. Write a mantra—a statement to help you move through the mourning… something positive.

   Mine, following the hit: This too shall pass. The question is will you help or hinder the process?

   What will your cognitive legacy be when it is over?

   Also mine, following the hit: I learned no matter how much I love and pour in, I cannot control, count on, or ensure someone else's love will be there. My own offering is freely given. However, I have a right to expect respect and mutuality.

CHAPTER 2

"THE HURT"

My joy disappeared that August night. The extreme suffering obscured my creativity, and it was nine months before I could again give birth to it. I was imprisoned within myself, and no, no distraction could seduce me from my desperate feelings. As time passed, I slipped into a more and more sorrowful place. I knew this was normal but that didn't help too much. It was a traumatic loss, and I validated my right to feel. At the same time, I resented what I had to go through. This laboratory was going to challenge all I was and knew.

The main difference between Chapter 1, "The Hit", and Chapter 2 "The Hurt", is the painful state only deepens. Family and friends mark "the hit" date from you telling them about it. Each has a watch set for an imagined healed date. You, on the other hand, can only keep marking time, parceling it out into hours, days, weeks, and years of torture, with eternity as the end point. Initially, the shock and numbness protect us from knowing the whole package that will be surrendered over time – a lifestyle with the beloved as with death, the loss of a relationship triggers ongoing reactions over time. Grief will not be deprived of a feeding frenzy. It is the price of attachment and disengagement.

Shame and Blame

I equated the initial months as being hit with a stun gun. There were feelings of shame at my own unacceptable feelings and limitations, not to mention the shame produced by an enhanced awareness of how humiliating and infuriating vulnerability could be. At least I had no tendencies to self-endangerment. Homicide, I must admit, would have been a choice long before suicide. Neither was there a lingering thought of hurting myself or others. If I'd suspected any of this, I would have sought professional help, as anyone should.

There was an adaptive denial that was building drop by drop in a puddle of truth. Often our brains try to spare us the shock of a traumatic event by slowly permitting the real truth to sink in. I navigated through and around it until I owned the one truth that was most painful: I was the un-chosen. He was gone from my life. My survival was in my own hands. The unimaginable pain that took my breath away, coupled with self-pity, came from resigning myself that all hope of a future reunion was past.

Amazingly enough, I was able to separate my professional life from my personal life and work. Looking back now, I see my incredible sensitivity and conscientiousness to and for my clients grow stronger in spite of my state. A death brings compassion by others, at least for a while. But divorce is so common that even unwilling victims gain little empathy. We've all heard those rational, even self-righteous words of the untouched: "I wouldn't want to be with someone who doesn't want to be with me". I've heard this often enough from clients whose friends are tired of hearing about it. Such words and the attitude behind them only escalated my internalized shame and embarrassment.

How can a significant other be so easily discarded and replaced by a so-called significant other whose behaviors are untested and lack time-tested and sometimes fire-tested credentials? And, if a sixty-five-year-old woman in our society like myself believes she can readily find a replacement partner, she's not facing the statistics. The global impact on both parties is revealed over time. Each may choose another partner who will now be a part of family events. Divorce may not end relationships with all family members. Hurt feelings can be resistant to self-soothing and may result in depression and anger towards each other. The fantasy is, I'll now be with a perfect partner, happy ever after. The reality is all partners, including myself, are imperfect! Even if both parties want the divorce, the reality is far from the fantasy.

Containment

I needed an attitude adjustment. I truly believed my intellect and emotional state were too accurate for the task of healing. I remember learning that normal, good, mental health is somewhat of a distortion of reality. In other words, we have to convince ourselves we're safer than we are in actuality to leave our homes and take on even simple risks. Unfortunately, mental illness often renders an individual incapable of a healthy distortion, allowing anxiety and fear to take over. Somehow, for my self and my practice, I needed firm containers to enhance my self-belief: First, the pity party, then the rebirthing party, and finally the celebration party. A tall order, but a plan. In spite of myself, and against all objective evidence, I could not and would not surrender my hope. I kept slipping back and forth into my cocoon and setting the table for my pity party. The incredible competing thoughts and feelings of over-idealizing my husband and suffering forever plagued those early days. I dreamed of ways he and his lady lover could die. But then within minutes, slightly superstitious at my violent fantasies, I'd remind God of how psychotic I was and to ignore any requests coming from my irrational mind.

In my practice, I deal with inconsolable nostalgia where victims cannot complete their mourning and have surrendered their lives to nothingness. Meanwhile, their lives moved on after choosing the same type of mate or the opposite, often ensuring future failure. I have always encouraged clients to mourn past and present losses before constructing future memories. It is a restructuring process; Settlage in *Inner Torment* 1993, (p. 474) reminds us that healing requires both inner action and negotiation. We shuttle back and forth reweaving our past, correcting misperceptions. In time, there is a realization that I am not a bystander but a co-constructionist. This understanding can lead to forgiveness of both the self and others. I can "negotiate".....trade off.....my own imperfections for those of others, instead of opting for depression or isolation authoring the marriage.

I didn't want to be alone. I would have fought "tooth and nail" to keep him, but had been summarily erased like I had never existed. There was nothing and no one to fight. For all my excellent coping skills, I hurt so much. Everything outside of my professional life was a challenge. I had to take my life back from the broken relationship. My heart hid out and wouldn't speak, and my brain operated 100% of my working day.

At the close of the day, I lit my candles and mourned for the marriage I wanted and needed. But there was no retreat into a fantasy life. I wanted back the one I had—that was my best fantasy! I wanted to slip through the looking glass and stop the tragedy . . . so unfair, undeserved.

Alone Again . . .

All my life I've struggled to maintain my sense of self within a relationship. The over-giving, over-pleasing, and creating dependency never worked. Underneath was hostility when my own needs were not met. The little girl inside wanted protection and safety at the expense of emotionally standing tall. Unmet early needs keep vying for attention and are unrealistic. The parental home is where those needs are satisfied and not in a marital relationship. If the therapist is carrying similar baggage of this kind as the client, the therapeutic corrective experience needed for damaged relationships could well be interfered with.

My practice was primarily individual, 80% involving bereavement or divorce. I had always gone to great lengths to encourage couples to explore their relationships, reminding them that separation and divorce was often an option not a mandate. My professional self remained at the helm, carefully following therapeutic menus and screening for possible problematic counter-transference, where the therapist's responses become emotionally triggered by what the client is saying because of the therapist's similar personal issue or involvement. In counter-transference, the therapist is emotionally involved in the therapeutic interaction and can examine his/her own reactions and learn how others treat the client. The focus is on recognition and how it is dealt with than attempts to eliminate the counter-transference. Counter-transference is a given, but the quantity and quality of the interaction and hidden agendas can hijack the therapy.

During that period, recognizing my vulnerability, I opted to not begin new divorce or marriage cases. Those ongoing were well compartmentalized, and I did not want to risk contaminating any new clients with my own issues.

I Opened My Own File

After hours, I was taking care of myself as much as any client. No one knew how wounded my reflective side felt, as my core remained strong and steadfast. That core me grew up from and endured a stressful childhood, used meeting achievement needs for gratification. The reflective side contains mental representations of the family, friends, and acquaintances, who played some part in my life. Because of the early disappointments, my mental representatives—images of others when they are absent—have been less stable. It has taken inner work to reinforce those images and feel cherished with absences. At times, I seemed to be two people, the one whimpering and wounded, wanting only to hide under the covers, and the other the stalwart professional, absorbing clients' painful outbursts and silences and guiding them surely, a solid pilot. Almost like a detached observer, I marveled at how well I was able to both motivate and contain myself. And, why not? In excruciating painful states, my clients managed to continue to work and parent.

One of the things I missed most was my autonomy of thinking, feeling, and behaving a certain way. I was not my usual congruent self—more labile than I ever had experienced or known myself to be. It took a great deal more energy to work through the mourning, and I needed more rest in my off hours. "The hit" had fractured my heart. In those early months, it took all my knowledge of psychic first aid to make it through. I knew why, although knowing made it no less painful. My "attachment hunger" was in high gear, but as every professional knows, knowing—self-awareness—and being able to do something about it are two separate constructs. Giving him up was like surrendering huge pieces of myself. What would I have left?

First Resources: Others and Self

Initially, I isolated myself and relied primarily on my own resources. But my friend Sandie helped me move. My four adult children (Debbie, Ted, Cindy, and Terry) had rallied to my side, constantly calling and offering to help. The two living in the area were available 100% of the time. My friends, Gail and Bob, would drive two hours on the weekend and drag me out to dinner. And then there was Marvin – one of my landlords, who was so incredibly supportive (more about him later!). Ivan and Gene came to my rescue. I had a building of friends eager to share a cup of coffee. Georgette also listened to my tales of woe. Dr. Stan was only a cell phone call away.

Despite all these supports, though, I felt safer in my self-reliance. Seeing my children's pain quickly made me wall off the sorrow. I shared selectively and sought treatment only with myself. I had never had a drink, nor was I disciplined enough to take medications. My physical self felt weakened but capable of sustaining "the hit". I knew what a plus my starting position was, and it helped me hold myself. A trained bereavement specialist knows loss. I knew my isolation and self-reliance could join together and do the necessary work. So I convinced myself it was okay to withdraw and curl up in a ball. I was well aware of the psycho-analytic concept of repetition compulsion—the tendency to recreate a particular past situation in a marriage, for example, in the hope of fixing it in the present. Repetition compulsion can be detected in patterns of choosing the same type of individuals as those we divorced for our next significant relationships. This was not repetition compulsion.

I was dissecting everything I could, trying to blame one particular something, anything, which held the key to my recent abandonment. As a child growing up in a dysfunctional family blames his/her self, I tried to own what was not my fault. By treating my betrayal and rejection as a crisis arising from a single traumatic event, I was validating my loss with so much self-loathing. This was a terribly difficult situation: If you persist in taking over the 100% of the responsibility for your 50% of the marriage, you will absorb every untoward remark uttered by your rejecter, whose agenda may be obscure.

Earlier Losses: Trauma 101

I was aware "the hit" would have been difficult for anyone, but why was it so especially traumatic for me? I came from severe and persistent early emotional abuse at the hands of parents who were engaged in daily battles. I knew all the experiences had impacted negatively my capacities and defenses, my self-regulatory mechanisms, and my ability to analyze my environment and problem solve. I had worked on these issues prior to, during, and after becoming a psychologist. By recognizing the events of our lives that have negatively impacted our ability for self-regulation, we can work through earlier losses that continue to interfere with living life fully.

Total self-soothing was out of the question. My inner child had refused to work through the negative feelings of long ago. And so, they were insatiable and never gratified from without, but had been dormant for years. Now I was being forced to address all my losses...concurrently!

I have always been a work in progress. Now, I would be able to witness how successful this endeavor really was!

Thoughts and feelings are of course complex. Van der Kolk (1988) said the negative effects of trauma can be mitigated by two factors:

1. Preservation of an attachment system.

2. A strong belief system.

I thought of Benjamin Franklin's truism in *Poor Richard's Almanac*: "After losses and crosses, men grow humbler and wiser."

I knew true healing finally took place not with a fencing off or compartmentalizing the event, reactions, and actions, but with the ability to recall everything at will and close it out when I wanted to with little emotional discomfort, if any. In the earliest times, it is almost impossible to turn one's mind on to other concerns. As with any loss, the brain is obsessed with the hope of ridding itself of the loss and accompanying pain.

Post Traumatic Stress Disorder

I was engrossed in trying to regulate my feelings and thoughts in repetitively re-experiencing that first August night and the final January dismissal six months later. I was suffering from post-traumatic stress disorder, not from the drama of war or natural disaster, but from a quiet monotone-delivered sentence. And I was experiencing the effects of this disorder:

- Poor affect tolerance. Little things were triggering big reactions.
- Heightened aggression – my fantasies of my ex-husband and lover meeting violent deaths
- Hyper-arousal to mild stimuli – a drama queen on stage
- Irritability – My upbeat disposition was hunting for a tunnel to escape
- Chronic dysphoric mood – A pervasive feeling of helplessness was setting in
- Emptiness and inner dread – I recognized how disastrous this was to my being

After a traumatic event, we need to work on several areas:

1. Affect regulation – I forced myself to see friends

2. Impulse control – I resisted the temptation to do a drive-by shooting

3. Reality testing – I would accept that he would not change his mind and return. Slowly I would kill off persistent Hollywood scripts of a reunion

4. Interpersonal relationships - I began talking less about myself and listening to others.

5. Self-integration – I continued to read, learn, and grow, albeit in a painful state.

We have to get over the hurt. If you don't and continue to wallow, your bitterness will swallow you up. Death will hunt for you in the closet, and life will never even open the door!

Chapter 2
"The Hurt"

<u>Pre-Flood</u>

"What a recreation it is to be in love! It sets the heart aching so delicately, there's no taking a wink of sleep for the pleasure of the pain."
George Coleman the Younger, English Dramatist

<u>Post-Flood</u>

When one is in love one begins to deceive oneself and one ends by deceiving others.
Oscar Wilde
I think I'm beginning to get it.....not yet to accept it.

My Self-Portrait

Shock and disbelief played havoc with my heart. Time only deepened the permanency of the loss. Days and nights lingered on and on as every cell in my body ached. My brain sought a simple answer for the complexity of the loss. Healing the emptiness began when I surrendered to the pain and the unknown.

Lessons from Chapter 2

1. Time in and of itself heals nothing. It only gives you time to heal.

2. After losses and crosses men grow humbler and wiser.

Benjamin Franklin

Poor Richard's Almanac

(*For your refrigerator*)

3. For a while you feel numb, exhausted, and empty. Then the pain, suffering, and reality of the profoundness of the loss hit you. By owning all of this, one can work through the fears, anxieties, and depression, and reinvest. This tenet is the underlying belief necessary for reclaiming oneself and living fully. Begin to make this a possibility for your journey.

Your Self-Portrait

1. Identify fears, anxieties, or any depressive thoughts. Write them down in your journal. Challenge your thinking and feelings with other possibilities. Example: irrational thought.

   "I'll never find anyone else who will love me and not betray me."

Challenge: There are many people who like and love me. I need to stay in the present and work through the loss.

Your list:

2. Maybe

   Instead of blaming a wayward mate and waiting for that person to treat you better, it is time to own yourself. Accept ownership for all your feelings and hurts. List the top three of question 1. How can you soothe yourself? Throw your arms around yourself and commit to the healing process.

3. Write your new story, including a goal you might realize, even if you are alone. Savor the possibility of new dreams and new pathways, even though you are hurting. Future memories can help as heal in the present.

Post-it

When a lot of remedies are suggested for a disease, that means it can't be cured.

Anton Chekhov

(No wonder there are so many books on lost love.)

My Post-it

The wrong I suffered is not the only wrong wrenching my gut and heart. All my losses have formed a chorus that refuses to be silenced. I can choose a refrain to listen to in honor of my losses for now. I am changing and will continue to heal and grow if I encourage the process.

CHAPTER 3

"THE HEART"

I was heartsick over my separation and later divorce from my partner. Levin (1993) refers to a special kind of wound that goes straight to our core as being a narcissistic injury. Emotional responses include hurt, shame, and rage. Our self-esteem is lowered, and this blow shakes our confidence in establishing and maintaining a loving relationship. Although I was very familiar with the ways we view being in love and in a loving relationship, now I found myself delving into what the experts say with a passion I hadn't known for a long time in my marriage.

Coupleship

Welwood in _Challenge of the Heart_ (1985) says couples now face "a historic challenge . . . to find a synthesis between the need for belonging or commitment and the need to be true to themselves as individuals, honest in relationships, and respectful of their different growth". This challenge was certainly part of my dilemma, although I didn't even know it was.

Perhaps I subscribed to the myth, as so many girls are brought up to believe, of two hearts beating as one, living in the happily ever after. More than perhaps—naïve would have been a step forward. And yet, today power struggles and the fear of a broken heart keep some from legalizing their relationship. In non-marriages as much as marriages, the interpersonal relationship issues, financial issues, and heartaches when breakups occur are often Identical to those of a marriage ending in divorce.

Why have long-term relationships become too difficult? Forces of disintegration abound in our culture, where formerly the marital relationship was experienced as sacred. The nuclear family was surrounded by an extended family and supported by faith-based institutions. There was no concept of the family as an independent, autonomous unit. Marriage united communities and families and was often arranged for financial and social advantage. The present emphasis on individualism has influenced a couple's ability to negotiate the individual needs and manage marriage needs. This, coupled with a society that dilutes the value of commitment and intimacy, has contributed to fear, avoidance of commitment, and intimacy.

My own regret has been my inability to sustain a life long partnership with all the ingredients of a good marriage. Over investing in the other is probably as much of a mistake because you by nature under invest in yourself. The good enough relationship would encourage individual growth and new learning as well as in the coupleship.

Anatomy of My Marriage

My relationship may have been unconscious, but I was not. I was in touch with myself. No one would have assigned "cheater" to my husband. He was the model of proper behavior. Consciously, I knew the areas we avoided. I was in denial, and unconscious in thinking they were insignificant. I serviced my relationship fully, appreciating all the years I was privileged to enjoy. That's what hurt the most: my attentiveness just wasn't enough to make my husband happy. What I thought I had was a rich bank account of feeling full, {which would help me contain myself once I was able to accept the dynamics}. By serviced, I mean I yielded the television remote control willingly, deferred to decisions about meaningful areas, and basked in my contentment. I was unaware of how much of my joy was other dependent. The marriage gave me a feeling of being fulfilled. I could not face the rejection and fears of being alone. My ambivalence was the key to understanding how one minute I was in denial, and the next flooded with anxiety and fear. The flooding of emotions can cloud the reality; postpone working through the loss, and reinvesting in others who love us. On closer reflection, perhaps what I called love was the ability to hide out in my husband and in the marriage and maintain my own enchantment. Maybe this was what many wives did whose husbands suddenly announced after twenty, thirty years, they wanted a divorce. Maybe these wives were blind to their husbands' real needs or real selves, going along cooking and smiling, and not knowing their husbands' insides, or their own, for that matter.

Instead of a refining fire to grow in, it was more like a cocoon, protected from the outside environment. The relationship should have been a journey of a self-discovery, but I did everything to keep from undertaking it. I didn't know this until I begin the self-reflection. Caterpillars magically get pulverized and become butterflies. I think I was in a reverse metamorphosis. I was feeling pretty ugly, old, and un-cherished and nothing like a colorful, fun, winged, creature. I felt so un-deserving I lived without central air in a hot house for ten years. The house was not centrally air conditioned until his new love had her name on the mailbox. He called and asked if I wanted the coffee table from the living room that my mother had admired. He would sell it to me. He gave me her two chairs—freely—which was a kind gesture. He never gave me the duplicate key to my car. I hope one day he will pile all the Christmas decorations in that and not reside in his attic (he is Jewish).

Why didn't my relationship survive considering all I was investing? How could I have been so blind to his withdrawal of intimacy? Was it ever-present? I was challenged to explore what went wrong and what part I had played.

This truth was bitter and painful: if my partner desired to separate, it should have been my love and duty to "let go." But I created a door in my mind and opened it and placed my love behind that door, almost like a sacred chalice. As I've said, I truly thought in the beginning his decision could be undone. I locked it away in a corner of my heart, avoiding the truth.

Taking Responsibility

I found it easier to heal when I could go in and out of the door embracing my memories without flooding myself. This little fantasy helped me deal with the heartful of rejection. Being able to work through the loss in a more controlled manner was empowering for me. But my success was elusive for a long time. My heart refused to yield to my brain, which was very close-minded. "Let go"! my brain shouted, but I could not, or would not.

I was so full of "nots" . . . I was not going to move. I remember as a child standing very still thinking "This is a nightmare and I'll wake up." Now it was the same, but standing still was the last thing that would help. I needed to tell my heart to "let go" and give it up, over and over. He certainly used the "no" word frequently enough in the marriage. My husband loved dogs but decided we could not have one. My husband hated answering machines. That, too, was out. He told me when I was departing sometimes he just wanted to sit and have a few drinks (I never drank). I asked was that after 7:00-7:30 p.m. on Friday or Saturday night for he was always sound asleep.

I always like the program "Hart to Hart" about an attractive couple who solve simple mysteries in an hour program. My heart-to-heart talk show was replaying old episodes. New heart-talk would say don't draw conclusions about someone else's behavior without asking.

Triggering Old Losses

I knew all my losses were incomparable. As a psychologist too, I knew divorce has different effects on each sibling. All our abandonment issues from childhood continue to resurface until they have been worked and reworked and are no longer part of the unfinished business triggered by the separation or divorce. We may re-experience or avoid dealing with our losses. But more commonly, we go through alternating cycles of re-experiencing and avoidance. Our neurons record events, both cognitively and emotionally.

Over time, our feeling sets can split off from our thinking sets. Even in less extreme situations of stress, we are easily triggered and respond with more intensity than a situation would normally command because of emotional bone yards that contain residue from earlier losses. We often don't even know what these bone yards contain and they render the grief more complicated.

Therapy can help us face and reunite the early event components and let go of the painful state stored from childhood and now reinforced in the present. Avoidance only postpones the active pursuit of working through the negative events, and these "heart scars," as I call them, hang on and become triggered by present events long after the causal events are over.

I looked back on times when my husband had given feeble excuses for why he wasn't coming home on time. There were only a few over the entire marriage. I am so sorry for not honoring in others how significant that can become when the heart begins receiving messages from the brain. My heart recorded all the office phone calls if I was one minute late as he can hardly live without me. How dumb I felt later having told my friend and colleague Diane at lunch my marriage was a 91/2 perhaps 2 months before my termination letter!

When traumatic events appear to be over, the residual material in a matter of seconds take an elevator to free fall fifty stories, smashing our whole world. Because of our unique capacity to access the past and re-experience it as if happening in the present, our losses are resistant to willful commands. But the brain nevertheless wants to be done with the loss and forces us to focus solely on it until we finish the intense emotion and painful thoughts. It is taxing and unrelenting for anyone who has experienced a loss to complete the grief work. Bereavement for death and divorce places us in an exhausting process of mourning to let go of the sorrow.

Our society values productivity and happy campers. It has no tolerance for the bereaved. The message is: Get over it! But from the past sudden, negative, and uncontrollable events consume all our resources. Some of our most intense feelings are really attempts at forcing us to regain control and return to homeostasis. Sadly and gladly, we will never be the same individual after a traumatic experience. I've often pictured myself sitting in a church pew, in an age of innocence, thinking bad things happen to others. If I do the right thing, nothing bad will happen to me. When the first death of a chain of losses occurred and I had done nothing wrong, I recognized my own vulnerability.

My brain isn't sophisticated enough to assign labels to all my tiny and tremendous losses. It just links them together with all the healed and unhealed components. It is like pulling a train with a slew of boxcars. They are mine. I don't want to forget my history. I only want to continue releasing negative emotions that surround old events. The lessons need to be stored and filed in my learning library.

For me, perhaps framing my losses into a profession that deals explicitly with helping people deal with their losses helped me deal with the lack of control I experienced over personal losses. One can, however, in mourning choose many other ways to deal with it, especially avoidant ways. These are commonly addictions, such as alcohol, drugs, sex, food, shopping. My own experience with bereavement, both death and divorce, has resulted in the same symptomatology, with a different set of healing tasks. I try to avoid anything to excess that would isolate and insulate me from my feelings and make myself conscious of the need to identify and process what is happening. (For example, too much, or too little food.)

43

My Childhood Revisited

In the first three years of life, we learn we are not fused with our mothers and we begin to establish a coherent sense of self. We are not equally endowed by nature, our environment, or events of our lives. As Masterson (1988) says, our unique qualities are supported by our parents in a safe environment that is manageable, intellectually exciting, yet emotionally secure.

When our needs are not met in childhood, we can experience problems in optimal distancing. We may either avoid intimacy and keep a large distance between us and others, or engage in clinging behaviors. Interesting, many couples contain one of each position: fear of abandonment marries fear of engulfment. Stemming from the deficiencies experienced in childhood, as adults we can keep experiencing separation anxieties and defend against abandonment, real or imagined, from our mothers or mother substitutes. This defending results in clinging behaviors. If mother was too needy and kept us too close, we may become afraid of being taken over or engulfed. So, in adult relationships, we may be attracted to someone who repeats our mothers' behavior or does the opposite and keeps us at an emotional distance. We have never experienced the "normal middle" and don't know what to look for.

When someone rejects us and our abandonment issues are triggered, our pain may become so intense we feel we are going to die. This feeling could very much replicate early childhood deprivations of not having physical or emotional needs met in an adequate manner. Some of the latest brain research proposes one can raise an attachment score in a positive direction—meaning perceiving yourself as feeling less abandoned—by partnering with a healthy individual. Howard, J., The Owner's Manual for The Brain, Bard Press 2000, Atlanta, GA (p. 437). Bloom, F.E.; Beal, M.F.; Krupfer, J.D. 2003 The DANA Guide to Brain Health Free Press, New York, NY (p. 131). Individuals with a false sense of self defend against abandonment depression in which Masterson identifies "Six Horsemen of the Apocalypse": Depression, Panic, Rage, Guilt, Helplessness, and Emptiness. These feelings can become unbearable in people with a severely impaired sense of self.

Regardless of whether you have left someone or you have been left, the real self feels constantly under attack. This perception may perpetuate further clinging or distancing in future relationships. If we don't deal with our present and last losses, we are doomed to repeat what we haven't faced and don't understand.

As I worked back and forth through years of losses, my own past rejections and abandonment issues became better understood. Gradually, they took their measured places as were part of my personal narrative and no longer interfering with my joy or creativity. The ultimate task is to continue to weave the traumatic event into the life tapestry, letting go of the misery and letting the joyful events help counter-balance the hurt.

As I began to understand my feelings in the context of the whole, I was helped to accept the loss in front of me. My world view had been severely challenged. I had poured everything into the Camelot I'd built, and now I was exiled. It was unbearable to feel so naïve and trusting while betrayal and sabotage were all the while sealing my fate: divorce. Oh, how this self-defeating thinking would continue to resurface! I had to relocate my heart, and it was suffering. Nothing kept my husband from acting and announcing as he did. No one has to operate from a value system if he/she chooses not to. But my dwelling on his actions only delayed my healing. Our healing is influenced by both our world view and the willingness to adapt and create new meaning in our lives. It takes real determination to refuse to wallow and swallow anger, hostility, and raging emotions, to let go of the incessant waves of rumination and regret, and project them into moving targets (i.e. others). I felt like I had outgrown a whole wardrobe of clothes and they were "let out" until the material was spent. The only recourse is to replace the old with the new. It means thought, time, money, and a loss of the old, comfortable things in exchange for the unfamiliar, strange, even uncomfortable more stylish outfits. But, if we want to not only survive but make meaningful lives, we must clear out our closets. My discomfort has led to an exhaustive quest of why I created so much of my own emotional discomfort. There was plenty from the rejection. But I took a long, long time to bounce back and reclaim myself. I long felt that I took much longer than I should have, given my profession, gifts, tools, skills, knowledge, and experience.

Self-Help

But I healed, and by many methods. One of the most effective was through using the tools of Rational Emotive Therapy to deal with my moods and emotions and regain control over my unruly emotional self. My heart-to-heart talks with myself continued to unmask my isolated self. In "I just can't get over it".....Matsakis, A. 1996 one discovery was how difficult it was to admit my loneliness and pain. I wanted to maintain the illusion of being invulnerable to life's losses, mostly to myself. Admitting the depth of my hurt was the first step to resolution. I also resisted journalizing. How glad I am I broke through my negativity and started writing. It saved me from the insanity of thinking I was unique in creating a total fantasy marriage.

Without more understanding and utilizing my skills, the deprivation I was experiencing would hold me a prisoner, wallowing in a cesspool of negative emotions. By prolonging the fantasy that he might return, I was alternating between self-pity and the fear of uncertainty. By accepting his dictum I felt I was accepting resignation that I was going to remain in a sad way forever. Divorced meant embracing a new pathway and relinquishing the heartfelt one I had embraced. Perhaps, my entitlement program had developed unconsciously that if a stable marriage was what I wanted and I poured everything into it, it was a given that I would reap what I sowed. I'm referring here to a strong belief system that what I do absolutely gives desired outcomes. I'm repeating myself but that's what we do and the challenges to our distorted thinking need to be as persevering

But planning, thinking, and pouring in do not ensure the marital outcome one wants. Intellectually, I know and reason. Emotionally, I dismiss!

For emotion to influence health, it must affect the physical body. There are many ways this can happen, but there must be a physical impact of an emotion for it to alter physical health. Initially, I felt my body had shut down too much for anything, including germs, to enter. Later, I'd feel my toxicity was equal to any challenge. Initially, a pervasive denial of what was really truth produced "emotional toxins" that were insulating my being from the pain. As the levels rose, they prompted my self-help approach to lower the levels. Only much later would I begin to care for myself for the sake of my health. My emotions, including anger, fear, and distress, were in a sense health- promoting. They were playing an important regulating role, promoting overall functioning by insisting I work through this. But I needed to monitor them and ensure they operated inside a certain range or they might lead to disregulation and disease.

Depression

These are also successive steps toward letting go, with distancing being the most difficult for the unchosen or discarded one. In letting go, one endorses the solitary traveler, again, willing to embark on another pathway. Grief and rage may alternate with calm and controlled behaviors. The most difficult realization is the intense state of being home alone, and this can lead to traumatic depression.

In depression, one is preoccupied by despair, suffers appetite and sleep disturbances, psycho-physiological complications, and impairments in other functioning areas. Depression, often involving anger turned inward, can deepen, accepting the loss at some distance for a long time. Eventually, I realized my depressive symptoms, coupled with hostility, had to be explored. I focused on understanding, letting go of my rejecter, and began turning to others who desired my friendship. Reconciliations happen but infrequently, and by courting the rejecter, you place your life on hold. It takes determination and restraint to choose wisely when our hearts are obsessed and possessed with love.

Why wasn't I insightful enough, once the relationship had been killed, to see that it was beyond resuscitation? In part, because he kept inferring it might not be over. Often the beloved who has blown up the marriage has financial gain in repairing the relationship immediately. This is a ploy. There is no compassion and caring in this situation that is strong enough to sweeten the cesspool of poison flowing from the cover up. The beloved may keep pulling further away, often preferring lies and deceit than the truth, under the guise of sparing your feelings. The lover begs, pleads, and tries to bargain with someone who is unreachable. Thus, depression deepens.

Help from Therapy

In therapy, both partners have to let go in different ways. The relationship is not ended by divorce or death. Feelings have to be worked through as the ties are broken. The longer the marriage, the more complex the thoughts and feelings for both partners. Breaking up can resemble giving up an addictive substance, such as cocaine.

A poor marriage is like a starvation diet. Crumbs may seem like a full meal. The ties are not equally valued by each partner, and the one leaving may still

47

desire a sexual relationship or friendship with the one left. This rarely makes sense to the one betrayed and abandoned. He/she may capitulate in hopes of reunion, only to be abandoned again and again. What keeps the unchosen from leaving? Perhaps the emotional ties, fear of being alone, economic concerns, and the shame of divorce. Many couples have chosen to stay together for the sake of children and/or religious reasons in a physical on site roommate status. Emotional shackles are resistant to change.

Often, therapy can be a safe place to explore "patterns of picking partners" who fail to measure up to an emotional construct we have long harbored. Support groups can help us remember the terrible history of the relationship as we over-idealized the spouse. They can also help us rebuild our shattered lives.

Halperin (1982) enumerates the three major tasks necessary to further the goal of leaving a relationship:

1. Recognize and free yourself from "attachment hunger" feelings that are keeping you from leaving.
2. Recognize and put a stop to the specific self-defeating mental processes that keep you immobilized.
3. Regain and maintain your sense of identity and self-worth without the attachment-fetish person.

I knew by expressing hostile and jealous feelings candidly, directly, and spontaneously it would be valuable. It was a little late in life but still necessary for me to release my feelings. Outbursts can help a child learn to control negative feelings if a parent is tolerant. I also knew my marriage had provided a safe haven for many years. I was better for it! I was faced in running my whole life back through a videocassette to deal with the painful abandonment. I was punished for my negative thoughts and feelings as many children were growing up in the 1940's-1950's. My irritable nagging and critical mother (due to her own personal problems) was incapable of providing a secure, mirroring environment that would have helped grow a more secure individual. We seem doomed to repeat what has not been remembered, reflected upon, and worked through.

But I thought I had it right! My life had seemed happy. Attachment is but one factor in emotional life. But it is the important key to understanding ourselves.

The Role of Hate

I struggled not to hate my husband, who had unilaterally, without anticipatory warning, blown up my world. I hate to admit this, but in the beginning, I hated him for what he did, how he hid out, removed himself by engaging in an elicit relationship, dumped me overnight, forced me into surrendering a home we shared, shattered our lifestyle, and tore apart my dream of walking hand-in-hand into the sunset on Palm Island. This scenario was so stuck in my conscious and unconscious minds that I couldn't bear the thought of any of them.

I include hatred as a major motivator in grief work. Most of us find hate repulsive, even if we feel that the other is deserving of it. But our hate is fueled by our longing for union and continuing to blame the other for leaving. At the same time, if not channeled, all, include hating the hater, is most destructive.

Hatred is incompatible with our value systems. It binds energy needed to create a "new ancient pathway" not focused on materialism but on more spiritual pursuits. Look at what hate does: If I can't let go, I must have turned him/her into an emotional supply store. Whatever I thought I had has now disappeared, and hatred dwells in my past and rents space in my head. A thief, it plans revenge in the future and steals my present.

J. Ruth Gendler's *Little Book of Qualities* (1984) has a wonderful passage on the all-consuming negative emotions. She speaks of jealousy, but we can easily substitute hatred:

> Jealousy stands by the blue flame of the gas
> stove stirring obsession stew. In his mind he
> is tearing people limb from limb. He wears a
> shirt that is almost in style with its odd angular
> shapes and bright edges. He can be quite
> charming when he wants to be. He certainly
> has a flair for drama. After a while, though,
> the roles jealousy takes begin to seem shallow,
> dishonest, and repetitive. The more upset he
> feels, the more loudly he denies it. For a time,
> I stopped giving parties because he wouldn't
> come if I invited certain people. At that point,

I couldn't give a party without inviting him, and
I was unwilling to censor my guest list for his
sake. He is quite capable of showing up
anywhere, unexpected, uninvited, unwelcome.

The role of hatred in healing is first to admit it and, second, to see its destructive role. Then we can choose to let go of what has abandoned us and reinvest in the rest of life that awaits our attention.

Regrets and Fears

It isn't the burdens of today that drive people mad. It's regrets over yesterday and the fears of tomorrow. Regret and fear are twin thieves who rob us of today. Psalm 118.24 asks us to turn away from both yesterday and tomorrow, telling us: "This is the day which the Lord hath made. We will rejoice and be glad in it."

By integrating our understanding of our childhood and how we defend against abandonment depression, we can begin to exercise more control over our assessments and decisions. Resiliency is the ability to rebound and live fully in spite of negative events that we have little or no control over. A belief system that precludes passivity and is task-oriented can help minimize a harmful impact on the core self. Van der Kolk in *Psychological Trauma* (1987) points out that the less avoidance, social isolation, and depression we subject ourselves to, the better the chance for positive outcomes.

As we develop greater internal locus of control, we develop specific skills for specific situations. An internal locus of control is a perceived sense of control of being capable to take responsibility for my actions. We learn not only from our mistakes but also from our accomplishments. Individuals with external locus of control are more vulnerable to outside circumstances that render them feeling helpless, hopeless, and hapless. I experienced myself as internally controlled except within my marriage.

As Anderson points out in *Emotional Longevity* (2003), if we can understand and reframe our pasts in ways that are less of an affront to our well-being, they are less emotionally jarring and psychologically scarring. According to research cited by Anderson, explanatory style can predict illness, longevity, and immune status. Optimism is hard-pressed to give up but remains resilient, even In the face of paradox, believing events will turn out good in the future.

This thought was my life raft! I refused to believe there was no hope for recovery. I waffled and wallowed, but held fast to this premise. I had finally faced the reality of "the hit" but also had a plethora of "savings accounts" I could draw on from the past where misery had lost the battle.

Yes, my thoughts would sometimes hamper my motivation. I had to persevere in finding creative ways to heal myself, despite my negativity surfacing and resurfacing. Pessimists use self-blame and flagellation to punish themselves, which prolongs the hurtful state. They feel "lucky" when good things come their way. Optimists believe more in their ability to impact their own lives in positive ways.

Marianne Williamson in *Illuminated Prayer* simply and beautifully summarizes the relationship we have with ambivalence and the pull of pessimism as well as our yearning for optimism, and the help we need:

Meditation

Dear God,

Please lift the veil that separates me from the heaven which lay beyond.

Renew my thoughts so full of fear and judgment and the illusions of the world.

Renew my heart so burdened by the sorrows of the past.

Renew my hopes.

Chapter 3
"The Heart"

Pre-Flood

The heart has its reasons which reason does not know.
Blaise Pascal

Post-Flood

There appears to be a ten-mile life line between my brain and heart. The two have never been so far apart.

Myself Portrait

My heart lay under siege not by my husband but by myself. It was an autoimmune disease...an attack from within that had to be stopped. My emotions were out of control, responding to irrational fears and anxieties. I was not immune to the suffering of my broken heart. It would take a survival plan and a faith-based armor to guard against my self-injurious shadow side, unleashed in the chaosis.

Lessons from Chapter 3

1. Hearts are more reactive than active following a breakup.
2. Knowing is not the same as doing. Often they are quite a distance apart.
3. A person with a patient heart has always some kind of hope the future is better than the present.
4. The Chinese symbol for crisis is danger and opportunity.
5. Our hearts are not paragons of frankness. They are preprogrammed by culture, biology, life experiences, and loss. One needs to listen to thoughts and feelings, but only operate out a value system. Even that gets molded by one's autobiographical self! It is just more stable and trustworthy.

Your Self Portrait

1. Close your eyes and quiet yourself. Listen to your heart. Write what it is telling you. Now, ask your brain to comment on what your heart has spoken. If there is any action to be taken, write your long held beliefs on the topic at hand. An integration of thoughts and feelings can be asking your value system where to go from here may be most enlightening.

2. Accept your state of loss but not the permanency of it. Chart where you were feeling and thought wise when you were left. Make a list of "baby steps" to move to a new pathway.

3. Remember the heart links to your center and draws strength to help you move through the labyrinth of fear.

Post-it

When your heart is broken your boats are burned. Nothing matters any more. It is the end of happiness and the beginning of peace.

George Bernard Shaw

My Post-it

Following a heart attack one needs to ask for support and help. A broken heart aches for comfort.

CHAPTER 4

"THE HELP"

Initially, I was reactive and living in sorrow. At some point, I realized my feelings would never let go as long as I allowed them to flood my being. It took treating myself as a client and "charting" my own course. In therapy, I coined the word "happens" to represent all the facets of investigating where self-help, outside help, and helplessness converge. I would like to share how this simple framework helped me organize my world.

I let each letter of H A P P E N S represent an area or facet of my being that made a contribution to my self-healing

H – History (from womb to tomb-childhood until present)

A – Affect (feeling states)

P – Personality Profile (both positive and negative)

P – People in My Life (social relationships that work and didn't work)

E – Events (negative and positive)

N – Needs (includes wants and expectations)

S – Spiritual Issues

I assigned numbers to the significance of each area and how I was doing in each of those areas. I divided the areas into the ABCS: Affects

Behaviors

Cognitions

Spiritual Issues

I used the scale 1-10 to represent how functional/dysfunctional or significant/insignificant the area was initially. At the end of each consecutive year, the scale was used again.

History

Abandonment Issues:

Significant impact on ABCS (Affective, Behavioral, Cognitive, and Spiritual states)

Mainly a partner relationship significant on PRESENT divorce status

Initial response: Poor 1 – 2 (out of 10)

Current (four years later): 8 out of 10 scale

Goal: Self and other forgiveness

My numbers changed in all the areas from 2's & 4's to 7's & 8's over time. It is a continuing learning experience and creative endeavor to focus and address inner world instead of outer world issues.

Initially, all I could do was to contain myself. There was little understanding, empowerment, movement, or remodeling.

Although my heart work was essentially to survive "the hit", I needed more. I wanted to accelerate my recovery and began to feel whole. As I mentioned before, my joy had been robbed during the biggest hit – escaping in the first 60 seconds of that dreadful day. My biggest struggle was to accept that my love for my husband was unreciprocated.

In psychology, it is considered psychopathological to engage in a tenacious refusal to move on! As Kernberg, *Book Title* (1989, p. 190) points out, Unrequited love has seldom been portrayed as having a potential for growth. In neurotic borderline personalities and potential psychotic character disorders, love tends to intensify when it is not reciprocated. Individuals lacking object constancy [the ability to experience others when they are absent] are excessively dependent on external objects, especially others, for regulation of self-esteem and emotional wellbeing.

How did I manage to tackle the whole terrible scenario and move forward from victim to victor? What was causing my over stimulating, out-of-control existence? How could I deal with this unless I could make sense of why I felt tortured first by him, and then by myself. I struggled to make meaning out of the meaningless. I needed to be on a healing pathway marching forward. From womb to tomb, our emotional forces, love and hate, interact with our environment. How do we move toward mourning, acceptance, forgiveness, and growth?

Acknowledging my Fantasies

I never pleaded after the first time or two, tried coercion, or engaged in stalking. Please seek help if you are thinking about or engaging in these behaviors. That also includes murderous rage and suicidal despair. (I'm not referring to a passing ideation or entertaining the thought of purchasing a voodoo doll and sticking pins in it!) I was grateful my excess of optimism was resistant to reality that was impinging on my life. I felt horrible but never thought it was the prophecy of doom and gloom forever. Not for long did I have to deal with my magical thinking that he would drop by or call. As time passed, it was only too clear these things wouldn't happen as, after a time, my daily unstable moods melted. However, my realistic hope warred with my unconscious denial based on unrealistic hopefulness. What seemed to fit initially was the character armor excessive hope provided that kept reality at a distance. I recognized that this self-protection was self-editing and controlling truth so I would not lose myself. I was willing to tolerate any current suffering that Inner Torment described. But the horrible truth is that excessive hope only fuels narcissism and strengthens and prolongs the hidden masochistic suffering of the injured party (Inner Torment). Often the ex-partner-to-be promotes these false hopes in the other for narcissistic or divorce settlement needs.

In therapy, clients reflect on "some day" – a time in the future when one would be completely peaceful and conflict-free. Pining for a lost love is common in all forms of bereavement. A healthy self creates an atmosphere of emotional security and acceptance. This holding environment is internally consistent and helps us live fully, soothing ourselves when losses occur.

Fantasy in Both Camps

I know now it was the staying power of my marriage that was missing. We didn't have a relationship with continual discovery and the ability to confront and grow. Adaptation was absent because our hearts never shared. Mine would have said how insecure and fearful it was to not be the beloved but to love so much in part due to attachment hunger. Who knows what he would have uttered? Our vows were more like "ows" for him. He had to have been somewhat fearful of losing his individuation since I valued the "coupleship" so much. I know now I saw myself more through his eyes than from my own. He wanted a child to direct and offered a trade of security and safety. He reasoned his lack of wanting a sexualized relationship would not hurt the marriage or me. He also held fast to the belief my work was psycho babble and that my feeling sets were unequal to his logic. He was wrong on all of the above. My endorsing his program reflected a partial surrender of myself. Why else would the recovery be such a heart challenge?

What I wanted and Needed

My inner child wanted safety and fidelity in the relationship. It wasn't looking for a parental figure consciously. I would have been hard pressed to hear the "I don't love you" prior to the bomb explosion. Perhaps he knew of my inability to hear and engage in a conversation regarding his feelings and desire to end the relationship. It would have left no choice but to blow up the relationship after he began his new love affair. He said, and I believed him, "if she or someone like her hadn't entered the picture, I would have stayed." I'm still not willing to entertain this discussion, even with myself! Only honesty and openness can be expected and accepted in truly healthy relationships.

Acceptance of our Difference

How do you balance love and individuality between two real people with genetics and histories and less-than-perfect parents to produce the necessary blend of mutuality and freedom? Each individual sacrifices a portion of individuation to contribute to the marriage. True vulnerability to another requires a great deal of flexibility and adaptation. Acceptance of our differences is a condition for forgiveness and freeing ourselves from a perpetual state of misery.

When love is amputated, joy and aliveness hemorrhage out. We close our wounds and the flow for self-protection often by a conspiracy of silence. We store our learning from traumatic events. Lessons can be valuable in the healing process. Our life tapestries need to be woven and rewoven to include the negative events.

It is the pain, suffering, and sorrow we work so hard to discard. Remembering it and re-experiencing it are not the same.

Surrendering My Fantasies

I knew divorce could strip away our personhood. We feel more like a possession than a person. Both the person leaving and the one being left have losses to work through. I must admit I had no empathy for my husband. It has taken a portion of self-examination to be forgiving and to understand the parting. No prediction can be made as to the favorable outcomes of one position over the other. The acceptance of the victim level by either party can leave one jaded about life.

Healing must be about suspending our judgments of each other and opening ourselves up to each other's being. We feel most loved when others recognize us and respond to us in a whole-hearted fashion. It is a painful truth that no one can give us all we need in just the way we want. The only way to wake up from the poverty of depending so much on others is to quicken our own tender aliveness and enrich ourselves in a variety of ways.

Bargaining with God for Relief

My grief at multiple losses has always taken the high maintenance road: suffering, working through, accepting, integrating, and moving on. But now, for the first time I was struggling with hostile wishes of revenge. The entire soap opera would automatically be televised in full living color in my mind, with me as the wronged party getting even. As my grandmother would have said, "You're a mess!" I wanted to hide from the story and the gut wrenching pain, but there was no hiding place.

I gave it to God.
He gave it back!
I knew He would help me with the work, but He wasn't going to remove this.
The mourning was mine alone.

Acceptance of the Ambivalence to Hurt, to Heal

At the core was my resistance to surrendering <u>all</u> hope for a reunion. I now had to consciously create self-helps to replace my soap opera that was playing unconsciously—full of distortions, guilt, and shame. My workshops on Job were followed by other spiritual presentations: *Desert Demons* (by William Kraft), Christian Self-Talk, and The Psalms and Emotions. I created them more for myself and shared my learning.

At times my emotions would run so wild that I felt barely able to regulate my physiological being. I would be overwhelmed, out of control, experiencing the intensity and prolongation of severe anxiety when I allowed myself to reflect on my position—unwilling to accept my reality. I was concerned that negative health outcomes would descend like the plagues of Egypt. My patience for everyday need-to-repairs was challenged. Living had to be the focus, with a conscious decision to promote inner peace a major goal.

Sometimes I would feel numb, feeling too cold, desiring to create a fantasy that "he is dead" to make the pain go away. I felt weak, ineffectual, and powerless, and tried to stuff the whole thing. I knew my immune system would take a blow—maybe a fatal one if I didn't become a better puppeteer. My stomach was too sensitive to medications to take any for much relief. What helped was my music, my books in the psychological literature and prayer, and most of all my journaling. I played over and over faith-based tapes, CD's, and my oldies collection. They helped sooth me.

For a long time, I kept looking to my husband, waiting for him to fix it. For months, I would be paralyzed on some level, not giving up the hope. No amount of advice, self-help, or prayer would move me from this steadfast position. But once the divorce papers were received, I owned the truth: cognitively: it is really over. Emotionally, I would not let go. Throughout my journaling and readings, I noted this firm position from an infirm mindset.

My Professional Self

I was fully functioning professionally, compartmentalizing and working through my sadness. Meanwhile, friends lost parents, and jobs, health, and life went on. I was careful not to take on other couple cases and shared with those I had only briefly. It was ethically a decision I made to give clients the choice to move on. No one did. I kept a healthy boundary—"I'd like to talk about me, but we are here now to talk about you". It relieved them of any feelings of guilt, although many sent cards. I later reflected on how glad I had been to make the decision to be upfront about my situation.

Exchanging Ambivalence for Hope

I started delving deeper to gain some understanding as to how my self-esteem could remain so high but my suffering at being left was so strong. I couldn't correlate the two. My marriage had provided a sanctuary—a place to feel safe, loved, and cared for. It wasn't the only ship in the harbor but a most significant part of my life voyage. This was a giant puzzle to be teased apart, understood, and released. I looked at the concept of "borrowed functioning" and reviewed what I had almost forgotten—we can make up missing functions by using a partner's strengths. He was grounded and seldom excited and emotional over everyday life. I was passionate about everything. If a fly crossed in front of my car, it was mine. Throughout the relationship, I became more aware of my feeling sets and able to contain myself. It was a healthy change that I continue to value. In the past I might have exploded over a disappointment. I was able to sooth myself in part due to my contentment and in part his example.

A Cognitive Takeover of my Emotionally Laden Self

My questions continued to mount, as I dissected the marriage—reflecting on how I felt. I began forcing myself to face the relationship in the here and now, not as I wanted it to be, but how it really was: unraveled. I continued to turn to knowledge and understanding through a multitude of self-help materials, running through a shelf of books on marriage and divorce. I was thirsty and hungry to devour anything and everything to enlighten my darkness and alleviate my pain.

A Great Marriage

My prior knowledge and voracious readings helped me see three necessary ingredients for a good marriage: communication, chemistry, and comfort. Good communication helps couples make up for "wished for" idealization. The waning of romantic passion is compensated for by the ability to negotiate boundaries, needs, and aspirations of each other. Compromises and adaptations replace the fantasy of having a perfect partner. Chemistry is whether and how you are attracted to the other. Comfort is the overall feeling of being loved and safe.

Dr. Judy Kuriansky in her *Complete Idiot's Guide to a Healthy Relationship, has* a series of tests that partners can take to create a good and lasting love relationship. I itemize them here with my summary assessments, from what I see now, of my own marriage.

- The thoughtfulness test. (We'd have passed with flying colors.)
- The unconditional love test. (He would have failed miserably. I'd still pass.)
- The security test. (We would have both passed—only I was deceived and living in a false state.)
- The compatibility test. (Good for both of us, or so I thought.)
- The communication test. (He would have failed this as well.)
- The commitment test. (Only I pass this one, obviously.)

More Learning

By the end of the first year I knew I had my work cut out for me. It was less about my ex and more about my next project, adventure, activity. I was still fighting aloneness and anger, but could find respite in others. And I realized how little I ever wanted to do without my husband. I can remember initially being too much in shock to recognize I was even alone! In a few short months, I would feel something of a mental dilemma:

1. To be intimate was to risk being abandoned.
2. To be alone was to self-impose abandonment.

I felt like going into hiding, and I did pull in and maintain a great deal of silence. My heart of hope needed space to slowly let go the Palm Island storehouse of plans and dreams. .

Obviously, when someone betrays you, "the hit" is so challenging to your defense mechanisms that this individual is experienced as bad, evil, or alien. A callousness develops about the person leaving that tear at the fiber of your soul. You keep thinking, who is this person? I can't believe how heartless he/she is.

The process of working through all the losses involved will tax the most adjusted individual. It is not the length of the recovery but the success of the recovery, and the willingness to reinvest in other relationships, that signal health.

Filling Attachment Hunger

The compulsion to remain connected, the intense craving, is so strong that it obscures the reality of what has occurred. A certain amount of attachment is normal in all of us in varying degrees, but when it becomes unhealthy it controls decisions that are not necessarily in one's best interests. This compulsion, attachment hunger, resembles an addition more than a loving relationship with mutuality and commitment. The illusion of oneness is so strong that it clouds good judgment. Halpern in *How to Break an Addiction to a Person* (1982) gives several indicators to show one is involved unhealthily and acting out attachment hunger that resembles the early relationship between mother and child:

1. No or limited free choice.
2. Compulsive nature to be available for phone calls, visits, and chance meetings.
3. Withdrawal symptoms.
4. A sense of liberation following the mourning period.

The addiction harbors a sense of incompleteness, emptiness, and a feeling of profound loss at the thought of being rejected and abandoned. The attachment hunger can be so strong, Halpern observes, that it can override judgment, control actions, and maintain a dysfunctional relationship to avoid the withdrawal symptoms. Good early attachment promotes roots and wings. Clinging in the present heralds the past faulty attachment rather than a reaction to the current relationship ending.

Not that it isn't wonderful to experience an overwhelming excitement at being in a blissful state. This state, coupled with "attachment hunger", can sustain one in satisfying both practical and infantile needs. According to Halpern, it represents a primitive dependency triggering our earliest memory banks. (Halpern, 1982)

How do we wean ourselves from this infantile-prompted state? Halpern suggests we make the "attachment hunger" more conscious, observe ourselves and our compulsions to jump to the beloved. As we become more aware, our infantile needs will fade and not engulf us. And then, current truths, newly discovered convictions, can then help prompt present healthier behaviors. In overcoming our addiction to another, letting go of the person, relationship, and lifestyle stems from realistic appraisal and a sound action plan.

Regressing

Halpern makes ultimate sense. I knew he did and yet I hurt so. Time was not my ally. It kept going, widening the interval of separation and compelling me to accept my reality, as painful as it was, and forced me to relinquish all hope. Would it really have mattered had he asked for a divorce with no one else in the picture? The presence of another, the superseding by another, felt like such a violation of my person. Now, thinking more about it and in light of more reading, I believe the loss was the hole, regardless of how it got dug. As with grief, it was the loss of my past, present, and future.

There are many losses associated with divorce, and not just the obvious material and emotional ones. Divorce can render you feeling disempowered. Your hunger for the beloved is impossible to satisfy in an earthly way.

At least anxiety over being alone has energy, and you can motivate yourself to make changes. But depression is stagnation feeding on nothingness. Guilt can result in depression because you feel so alone, naked, and unprotected. I was drained, overwhelmed, desiring only isolation and solitude. The only way I could let go and become whole—perhaps for the first time regarding the "attachment hunger" –was to sever all communication and visits with him. Although I wanted to be with him more than anything, paradoxically there was a comfort in being able to totally distance myself, and this replaced vengeance-seeking behaviors.

Differentiation: From a We to a Me Regaining Control

I speculated I would have to steal the control back from my emotions. In my professional capacity I easily accomplished this task with clients, encouraging their narratives and observations about them. I helped them separate their responses from the traumatic events of their lives. My clients shared stories of special occasions, weddings, vacations, company and school, tests, jobs, and going about daily routine that is so difficult to motivate oneself in the midst of sorrow.

Now I had to learn from them and become my own therapist. My personal task was to engage myself and do the work. This required a method for visualizing my set goal and excluding or containing my intense emotions from the loss.

I found myself jumping from left to right, up and down, in circles, desperate to regain control. I thought of a discomfiting fact: Our rate of speech is 150-200 words per minute to others. However, our private self-talk runs 1,300 words per minute! I was talking to myself at lightning rates, and none of my words were nourishing.

William Kraft in *Streams from the Desert* (2000) talks about the giant sequoia recording within itself the history of drought, flooding, and lightning, as well as normal growth. I firmly believe that humans too record all the scars and traumas. And the invisible scars are more dangerous than the ones we recognize. They bundle together to bring a deep sense of unworthiness, anxiety, and depression. Guilt and shame abound.

All losses involve change and all change involves loss. It would have been nice if I had developed a trauma package to pull out that Sunday evening in August to deal with my total disorientation and disbelief.

I built a container. I created a safe space physically and refused to be coerced into hating, hitting, or hurting anyone else. Initially, I tried calling in the troops. I knew of Johnson's observation in *Trust After Trauma* (1996): The intensity of the trauma's duration has less predictive value of healing than the ability to draw support from others, and I made use of many wonderful family members and friends, probably taxing their patience.

My children and close friends rallied to my side, but several individuals were a disappointment. I moved on, trying to accept the difference between those who genuinely supported and those who tried to talk me out of my feelings. I chose the time to work on issues. I collected little bits and pieces of inspirational poems and self-help advice Privacy involved not telling all or telling anything until I was ready. I continued to create doors to place painful subject matter behind. It is absurd to think health care professionals can take off weeks, months, or years to heal from traumatic experiences. Our tools are intensive and extensive and can be used in our own service during our private traumatic times. Seeking professional help was always an option for me which I didn't rule out. I kept a pulse on how I felt and whether I was drifting in client sessions. But my own trauma worked to my advantage. My work was so much on a conscious level and I was so committed that clients never had less than my best professional self.

Practical Suggestions

Surviving "the hit" with the lowest self-cost includes a plan. Keep it simple. If you can pare back on activities, you may be able to mourn more with less keeping up of pretenses. But you won't necessarily shorten the time.

At the same time, try to stay busy enough to have respite from the grueling work of mourning your loss. Work and regular duties can be a welcome emotional breather, but allow enough time to experience the painful hit. Yes, it is a juggling act, and one in which only you know the right times for each aspect.

Suicidal feelings and thoughts are not uncommon following a traumatic event. If you feel these intensely for long periods or they seem to control you, seek help from your spiritual leader, support groups (family and friends empathetic to your plight), and professionals, if necessary. Suicidal feelings and thoughts often emerge from the shame of being in a position of loss. Acknowledge your situation, use self-talking, and know suicide is a permanent solution to a temporary problem.

How do you deal with the intense feelings of anger, sadness, fear, anxiety, and hopelessness that seem to take over? Humans' emotions are very paradoxical. By owning your right to feel the way you do and beginning to address aspects contributing to the feeling, your suffering will weaken over time.

Most survivors engage, as I did, in some type of magical thinking that everything will someday work out. Couples whose marriages are in trouble may wait years to seek professional help, believing problems will disappear in time. And you've probably tried different forms of denial to avoid disrupting your mental representation that nothing was wrong with your relationship. Why? Because interpersonal conflict stirs up intense feelings of guilt, shame, rejection, and abandonment.

But time never heals wounds but gives us time to do our work. Hope has to be based on reality and not wishful thinking. I could still be waiting for my husband to repent and reconstruct our nest. That would be thinking like a dodo bird, not to mention cutting off any forward motion on my part!

Initially, during the survival state, it helps to develop a 911 plan even under duress. Early decisions can impact the intensity and duration of our mourning. Trauma challenges our personal belief system and forces us to revisit the existential questions: Who am I? Where am I? Where am I going? Later the question becomes, Where am I going to get the money from to go anywhere?

My first step was to review some of my self-help books I recommended to clients. They get better! First you just survive, then you examine what has happened, and then you begin to let go of the pain of what has happened. If the survival period was so rough and you were scared for your life, then the examination process is the gauntlet of exposing oneself to painful realities we have tucked away from self-awareness.

Grief is like waves that continue to pound the shore. In therapy, I use the word AWARE:

A cceptance

W orking through

A djust

R econstruct a new life

E xistential issues – of faith need to be addressed

By creating new meaning and accepting the suffering, we move the battleground to how to move into the future. Otherwise, the focus remains on the loss and the helplessness that accompanies it.

The initial shock and disbelief that my marriage was targeted sunk, and I was marooned on a raft triggered withdrawal and avoidance. Survival would include the total loss of a lifestyle and being uncoupled. I recognized grief was not a package and each thread would have to be reexamined. It would be an exhausting process to let go but I knew that was my goal. Only when I fashioned a new life would my joy begin to return.

It took everything I could muster to compartmentalize all that was happening and allow only one thing at a time to work on. My self-talk was running a mile-a-minute. I made no major decisions and adopted a holding pattern. Finally, toward health and reconciliation with myself, I chose to do the following:

- I accepted the painful state.

- I engaged in the mourning process of accepting what I could not change: I was not the "un-chosen" to the entire world, but only by him!

- I avoided whatever could be avoided and dealt with my intense feelings and sufferings.

- I prayed. I had others pray for me without knowing much about the situation.

- I made no life decisions that could be postponed.

- I forced myself to exercise, pay bills, and work by compartmentalizing various scenarios related to the situation.

- I utilized all my learning, experience, self-help materials, and music.

- I began collecting affirmations.

- I turned to God. My Bible was a resource for inspiration that suffering is human and I could work through this "desert experience."

Spiritual Help

My own protective rituals included journaling and lighting candles. My writings helped me reorganize myself and formulate a framework for facing my grief head on. My prayers were soon converted from "Fix this terrible thing" to "Help me fix my traumatized spirit struggling to emerge from this nightmare." I wore the jewelry, looked at pictures, and took my feelings heart-on.

My maternal grandmother was my spiritual guide. She never said an unkind word about anyone and was always reading her Bible. A large oval frame hung on her bedroom wall with a picture of her child, Ruth Helen, on her tricycle. She was one of six children and had died from an illness at the age of six. My grandmother had never healed from the pain and I vividly remember many times witnessing her tears as she gazed at that picture. Maybe she felt she was responsible for Ruth Helen's illness and death; maybe my grandmother never forgave herself.

Kraft believes that only through divine intervention, the Divine Counselor, are the wounds truly healed from the inside out. Satan's weapons include an arsenal of psychological afflictions, including fear, doubt, anger, worry, and guilt.

My spiritual self was appointed and anointed to engage in the heavy-duty heart hits. Four things were available at all times: The Word of God, my inner holy spirit, my conscious, and my ability to learn and discern the higher road and a new calling. Family was wonderful, some friends were too, but God was my only valentine. His availability is unmatched!

Learning from Job

From my own upsets I was reeling, rehearsing for Job's role, and facilitating everyone else's losses. My workshops on Job were both a challenge and a cache. I remember praying to God just before delivering one of them, "I just can't do this!" By the time I had dressed, though, I was calmer, and reaffirmed my commitment to myself. Our lives need to be preserved during traumatic times. My life was like a caravan, always in motion. I loved it and wanted it protected until I could pick everything up again. What could I learn from Job?

We read in the Old Testament Book of Job that he was a wealthy cattleman who lived in Ur. The story opens with a description of all family celebrations, Job's prayers, sacrifices to God, and how blameless and upright he lived. We are told Job is devout and prays to God for his children—in case "they have sinned and turned away from God in their hearts".

A dialogue opens between the Lord and Satan. God singles out Job as the finest man in all the earth. Satan retorts, "Sure, because he is so rich and protected by you! Take away his wealth and he'll curse you to your face." The Lord then tells Satan he could take his wealth but could not harm Job. And Job over time loses all his children, all his wealth, is afflicted with boils, and is in sorrowful struggles to make sense of what has happened.

His friends start out in mourning and empathy but do not maintain that posture. Each has an idea of why this is happening to Job. Job maintains faith but still has questions for God. God's answer is to appear to Job and let Job and us know how much we would like God to play by our rules and how impossible it is for us to understand life. God inspires Job to move on. So Job repents for his foolishness and God restores his family and wealth (twice as much!). God is furious with Job's friends and insensitive, inaccurate advice, and Job prays on his friends' behalf.

In spite of his difficulty understanding how terrible things could happen to an obedient servant, Job's biggest gift—and lesson to us—was his faith. He

71

exemplified the faith that God hears our suffering and will not abandon us, regardless of how it looks to others.

Spiritual Sustenance

In Max Lacado's book *It's Not About Me,* 2004, he writes: "Trying to make life all about us pushes happiness further out of reach." A "God-centric lifestyle" is his term for the freedom to live more fully in a spiritually- centered life. All else eventually fails us . . . people, materials, power, position. God remains everlastingly available. I knew this, even though I was still sad and sensing hope of reuniting slipping away.

In *The Legend of the Three Trees,* George Taweel and Robert Loss (2001) comfort us with the following:

Sometimes the dreams that we have

for ourselves are so much smaller than

the dreams that God has for us.

In the story, the three trees dreams come true, but not in the way they had imagined. And so it is with each of us. For if we follow God's path, we will travel far beyond even our greatest dream.

I turned to God, I turned to myself and tried to accept what was so painful to accept.

One thing that helped me greatly was imaging me talking to God, complaining about my abandonment and struggles. He would listen patiently as I complained about the one pot both chickens continued to fly out of. (Chickens could represent any loss.) The emptiness was so painful, I would tell him. And He would reply:

How sorry I am you are struggling and

struggling. I am here for you, Teddy.

What about the other four pots full of

double chickens that you still have?

I hated this dialogue! He was always pointing out all my other "chickens"--all my blessings and what was present. This exercise—mental imagery and the accompanying self-dialogue—saved me from overwhelming self-pity when my gifts and storehouses were still fully present. No one ever has it all for long. I was learning to appreciate my gifts—in spite of the immense anguish--all of them—and my history on a daily basis. It seemed so complex at the time, but simply stated, I gradually let go of "I don't deserve this—why me!" I accepted it as what it is. I needed to go back into my past, including my marriage, and understand my part, my lessons, and at some point let go of the pain. Otherwise, I could just give up; surrender myself, and all I could accomplish in my life. Perhaps that would only be loving others and being supportive. I didn't have to win the Nobel Prize to be worthy.

I continued to journal and now started to take over my emotions more and more. They kept lying to me and said "the hit" was the kiss of death. My hurt refused to recede. My heart was broken. My head was insulted but it was not going to surrender to the fearful, anxious, pitiful, purposeless little child inside me that was in excruciating limbo.

What did Job do? He prayed. He talked to God. He wrestled with his suffering. He refused to surrender his calling—to serve the Lord. Job was my role model. Of course God restarted his whole life and then some in Chapter 42.

Holy Bible NIV 1973, 1984, Zondervan Pub., Michigan.

With my spiritual self in charge, it was time for more action. Grief is reactive, whereas mourning is a more active state. Initially you can hardly move, but in time, you start taking baby steps. I would only feel alive if I could start examining what happened, let go, and move on. I kept repeating this statement like a mantra, clinging to it. I kept engaging in gradually more letting-go self talk:

I'm beginning to make sense of my heartache and to stop projecting all my unhappiness onto the betrayal. I'm afraid of all the changes that his choice to love another is requiring of me. These painful things are all fleeting thoughts and feelings. I'm reading, digesting, writing, and wondering about myself and what is yet to come. My movement from surviving to thriving is challenging and painfully slow. But I'm willing to examine myself more and find a new pathway. I am daring to dream of a new life. Lord, help me be the overcomer you've endowed me to be.

Looking backwards and forward for you the reader, I realize how I keep weaving back and forth. My healing was not in linear movement. As bereavement is experienced in waves, so is divorce. I've included this page to keep you focused on where I've come from, where I am and where I had to move to.

73

Part I – Surviving – My Reactive Self
Hit – Hurt – Heart – Help

Part 2 – Striving – My Active Self
Self – Examining – Letting-go – Seeking – Fashioning

Part 3 – Thriving (Both Reactive, Active Reflective)

My Transcendence:
- Palm Island
- Workshops
- Self-Work

Yours:

_____

_____

_____

Chapter 4

"The Help"

Pre-Flood

Well, now, there's a remedy for everything except death.

Miguel de Cervantes

Post-Flood

"Blessed is the man who expects nothing, for he shall never be disappointed" was the ninth beatitude.

Alexander Pope

Myself Portrait

Boxes of band aids to shut off the bleeding and a score of family and friends were essential ingredients in my first aid kit. I ran out of supplies. Myself was the last resource I turned to for total resolution. Clearly, I felt disenchanted and therefore dis-empowered. The epiphanies were slow.

The keys to unlock the suffering were in my possession. No opiate would substitute for a long term investment in self-help. I began setting new goals, new dreams in the midst of the agony. Both could exist later and I had a cognitive map written simultaneously. My spiritual self was the most trustworthy part of myself. Resistance reigned inside of me. First the sorrow, then the fear, then the baby steps, and finally three chapters on toilet paper. I could keep redesigning the rolls with minimum investment. Following a plan, I told myself, would be tomorrow's venture.

Lessons from Chapter 4

1. A support system is not just a group of individuals you know. It is a group "you perceive" to be supportive.

2. Time was not going to heal anything. I would have to invest myself in the process.

3. As time went on, it got worse instead of better. Grief is not linear going from bad to better.

4. In my most desperate hours, a new dream was striving to be born.

Yourself-Portrait

1. Call in your support team. Know who can offer support without exercising control. Thank everyone for advice and loving you. Save huge changes until you were back in charge of yourself. Journal your accomplishments and remind yourself of how you can move forward even in distress.

2. You are now your best friend. List your own helpful qualities. Make your map and know revisions are the result of choices.

3. Take a minute to reflect on your fears. They are still present...fighting to shut off your self-belief system. Confidence comes from trusting yourself and doing – not from plans alone.

4. Set one goal. Map out how you will achieve it. List fears and obstacles. Use your problem solving self to plan and execute. The failure is in not trying. Set small goals with small steps initially.

5. Always feedback to your heart and brain. Your accomplishments, self-talk is powerful and will encourage forward movement.

6. Who do you trust to give you honest feedback combined with empathy? (Maybe it will take a therapist.) Share your pathway.

7. Time to contemplate a new calling, dream, adventures, goals, and missions.

Post-it

Fools run in where angels fear to tread.

God helps those who help themselves.

Survival is not a destination. It is only a recovery way station.

I'm not challenged to survive. Participation in life, however, has to coax, prod, push, cajole, and drag me kicking and screaming. I know I keep saying I'll move when I'm ready. My ready is a procrastinator.

PART II – STRIVING

My Active Self

STRIVING

Introduction

There is no assurance, no matter what you do, that someone will not come along and seduce you or your spouse if conditions are ripe. A stellar performance evaluation is no guarantee of being kept out of the un-chosen pool in spite of past promotions.

I, along with my friends, saw my marriage as by all appearances high level functioning.

I'm pretty sure that was the case until someone took aim for my husband's heart. She worked with him, knew he was married, and laid claim to him anyway. Of course, he was 100% responsible for his infidelity, lies, and betrayal. He may have blown the marriage up unilaterally, but I admit he had to have been dissatisfied or less satisfied than he portrayed. I know now my hope he would return influenced making her the target for all the suffering. She scooted in, and I slithered out. She had a ready-made life—one I relished and was grateful for. As we exchanged titles, my life crumbled, my "self" emptied. I was in a serious loss. By the end of the first nine months, I recognized my nesting as narcissistic and rendering me devoid of motivation. I became entrenched in my safe office that had the potential for becoming a cave dweller.

The next four chapters continue the "self" model. The first four chapters (The Hit, Hurt, Heart, and Help), represent our positions in the earliest periods of loss—surviving being the main task. The next four chapters (Self-Seeking, Examining, Letting-go, and Fashioning) continue the action phase of moving on.

Chapter 5 – Self-Seeking recognizes the self in the marriage may have surrendered pieces essential to reclaim on the solitary journey. It offers a framework for self-work.

Chapter 6 – Examining, explores ways to assess our progress as we journey onward as overcomers.

Chapter 7 – Letting-go helps us release resentments and anger by confronting our fears and anxieties in their fullness.

Chapter 8 – Fashioning focuses on reinvesting in ourselves and others.

Part III will contain components of both in the task of "Thriving".

Self-Assessments

What can you do in the earliest hours of being in a 911 state?

1. Try to locate yourself if at all possible to an emotionally and physically safe space, even if for only a few days.
2. Do not move out of a home that is jointly or singly owned without seeking legal advice. State laws differ and you need to protect all your rights, even if you feel like giving away the farm.
3. List family and friends who will support you without being judgmental.
4. Call upon your minister, rabbi, or other spiritual individuals for support. Let your spiritual self seek comfort, support, and relief from God.
5. Do not make rash decisions. There will be plenty of opportunity to take action. Make a plan. Try to constrict your activities to focus on choosing a step-by-step plan for handling what is currently happening.
6. Act within you own beliefs, never allowing your impulsive self to be in charge. Know you will have time to make economic plans after you have pulled yourself together. Self-help materials cannot choose wisely for you and can only present possibilities for you to choose from.
7. When you begin to collect your thoughts and regain some element of emotional stability, formulate both short-term and long-term plans.
8. Keep contact to a minimum with your partner, even if children are involved.
9. Hold your tongue and avoid engaging in name calling and mud slinging.
10. Break off contact with ex-loves until you can compose and assess what has happened to determine a course of action.

CHAPTER 5
SELF-SEEKING

We are One: Two: One.....

Our culture promotes the romantic fantasy of melting and merging with a partner to become one, almost as if this is the only goal of life. Obsessive love, elicit relationships, and affairs, are presented as the norm, desirable, and healthy, and glorified in the media. A good enough marriage is as easily targeted by a seductive individual as a dysfunctional relationship. A break-up is devastating to one if not both partners due to the lengthy separation of parenting, affection, and property. This traumatic experience can block the capacity of our minds to adapt by inhibiting the process of integration.

Our minds develop in childhood within familial experiences. Impairments to balanced forms of self-regulation can be transmitted from one individual to another—parent to child—because we depend so much on our attachment relationships.

Marry to Heal Childhood Wounds

We often marry to fix early wounds, but this is usually an unsuccessful action. However, a grounded spouse can do much to provide a stable place where we can continue to grow. Therapy is about working with the complex mixture of feelings and defenses formed in response to earlier experiences of insecure attachment. An unwanted divorce strengthens all the fears and insecurities stemming from childhood. Future intimacy is related to the opportunity to embrace our loss, heal ourselves by working through and letting go of negative emotions and thoughts, and addressing earlier insecurities. Self-work helps us identify and address past hurts as well as present losses. It can also mask action if we deliberate in quagmire too long.

By promoting a more adaptable and flexible way of being within intimate relationships, we increase our chance of living fully in a more intimate way with many others. Failure in coming to terms with loss may result in permanent withdrawal from social relationships. This was why it was so difficult to take responsibility to heal myself. I thought he did it. I didn't deserve it. He needed to make it right. Crazy thinking! I was obviously not my husband's main course—more like his curse.

Our genetic inheritance contributes to our personalities and influences the limits of who we may become as adults. Emotionally unavailable parents produce clingers and avoiders. Clingers hurt from early abandonment and need constant attention and reassurance from partners. Avoiders decided the disappointments and hurts were so painful they would never be close to anyone again.

Both positions pose intimacy problems following divorce, for each is now reinforced. Wade Luquet in <u>Short-Term Couples Therapy</u> reflects on the fact we often marry people who are wounded in the same place as we are but have opposite energy levels. For example, one may be a couch potato and the other always immersed in activities. This may result in constant friction unless an understanding ensues.

Romance and the Dance of Intimacy

Romantic love is nature's tricky way of bringing two incompatible people together for the purpose of healing each other, and themselves. Not that each has what the other needs. Rather, what your partner needs is what you also lack and need to grow into. Often one person is overly energetic and social, while the other is a recluse. Both could profit from moving to a middle position, but this choice is more often passed over. Nevertheless, with good will and pride-swallowing and persistence, each can learn from the other and grow as necessary.

Star Struck

What if a new reality show was airing on national television and you received a phone call and this follow-up letter:

Dear _____,

Congratulations! Out of 10,000 letters yours was chosen to participate in our new reality series screening: Overcoming Divorce. Our television cameras will film your home, interview family and friends, and film your work environment, interviewing colleagues. Your letter stated you were recently divorced and are struggling to rebuild your life. We will film you now and air the initial episode and schedule sessions throughout this next year. Your progress will hopefully encourage our listeners to rebuild their lives following the heartbreak of divorce.

We will pay you $10,000.00 to participate in our show filming four episodes. Additionally, if you are able to detail your struggle, healing, and moving on, we will pay you an additional bonus of $10,000.00. Please reply no later than ten days from receiving this letter.

What is really at stake if you fail to work on yourself is lost time.....and very likely an angry life in which you contribute much less than you could otherwise. Too much of your psychic energy will be bound up in resenting, avoiding, defending against your hurt feelings and perceived hurts by others.

I wanted to turn tail and run back to the cave where I was safe. Oh, the world would have admired my 12-hour workdays helping others while I had only my professional hat to wear. Withdrawal was an appropriate response for I needed to care for myself after the breakup. However, those uncomfortable feelings that caused me to withdraw in the first place were very vocal. Unfortunately, I knew too much and had been too healthy to retreat for long. The fact was I knew I was worthy of having a life. It won't be a surprise for you who are dating to know narcissistic individuals also have low self-esteem. So do those who turn to favorite addictions.

I'm describing a self-seeker as a person willing to confront fears and anxieties experienced from being alone after being coupled. Myself needs my respect and attention including self-soothing to continue to seek a new pathway. I will have to confront my shadow side that wants to give off negative messages I heard during the breakup.

I hid parts of myself that aggravated my husband. He couldn't stand mail addressed to Dr. Teddy Tarr. He would remind me I was not a doctor—a psychologist, and had a doctorate. Oh my, I hid that title!

Fortunately, I had never referred to myself as doctor in my office, although I certainly had a legal right to as a psychologist. I would tell my clients Teddy, please, just Teddy. I always called my clients by their first names and preferred the same. I joked once in a workshop God would call me by my first name. (Probably essential after a series of failed relationships!).

<u>Alone Again</u>

Of all the problems associated with divorce, the loneliness has to be one of the most difficult for most of us, including myself. I tried to own my feelings and accept what I couldn't change. Sometimes, I made plans for dinner—an hour or two. At times, I would watch a DVD with a friend. By facing the loneliness, it became less powerful. It was tough to admit I likely would spend the rest of my life alone.

I thought of my grandmother widowed in her 40's or 50's and living until the age of 86. She never dated. I didn't know enough to ask her how she felt.

What strikes terror in my heart is how well I can do the lecture and how hard it is to pass the laboratory of life when it comes to marriage. How do you know if you are loved? What works for me may not work for you. My emotional being has to be as significant to you as your intellectual side. In fact, people who intellectualize may keep someone at a distance using reason and analyzing everything to do so. Often, the partner looks at other connections with envy. However, they are often temporary or superficial and have a pseudo quality that does not resemble intimacy.

B. Collins (1997), in <u>Emotional Unavailability</u> notes five boxes of emotional location, four of which are dysfunctional. We make choices of which box we want to operate out of for reasons mostly to keep feeling safe (in control). Unresolved issues and losses of childhood influence our choices. Control is a gratification focused position. It is a battle of wills and unsafe for both partners we can choose to move.

It is better to recognize past positions and make changes to become the problem solver now. It will help to look back on the marriage and own parts, roles, and positions you now recognize are less than healthy. (If you need additional help, I recommend reading <u>Emotional Unavailability</u> and seeing the role you played and not only blaming your partner.) Otherwise, we are doomed to repeat our mistakes.

The last area I want to address is self-structures. Expression of our emotions comes in part from parents modeling appropriate responses to events. They help us understand the significance of certain events. Parents also model the use of problem solving. Growing up in an angry household may promote an angry child and later adult. How parents expressed themselves in our presence makes unique contributions to our preschooler developmental phase. Punitive parents help children socialize in far less positive ways. Emotional competence is in part biology and in part learned.

My household was chaotic with a prevailing angry, hostile, parental relationship. I preferred to live at my friend's home. This could have never been declared. Rather, I took on excessive household chores to gain privilege to be distant— neither seen nor heard. Grades were important, so I performed academically and socially. Achievement and emotions were linked from the time I entered school. I remember many screaming bouts in adolescence, and being punished with switches, a slap across the face, and untold restrictions. Most of those I learned could be manipulated with pleading and perfectionism. My sister paid me to eat her unwanted food. Later perfectionist tendencies would result in self-attacks. I learned to work through much of this and enact changes in my thinking. With the breakup surfaced the residue of not being good enough. Being rewarded for our achievement is not such a bad thing.

It just mixed two areas related, but not mutually dependent on each other. Acceptance of academic failure (which I didn't have to confront), would have led to a hard hit to my self-concept. I had a right to my feelings and not blame myself for all untoward events that came my way. Nor do I now take over responsibility for not being able to change my moods instantly. I've learned to have patience with the healing of my losses.

Emotional regulation occurs in part through self-talk. In childhood, emotions may be stressful and flood our awareness. We learn to down-regulate our emotions in many ways. A working definition of emotional regulation is found in <u>Emotional Development in Young Children</u>, Denham, S.A. (1998), Guilford, N.Y., NY, p. 150.

Emotional regulation consists of the extrinsic (outside us) and intrinsic (inside us) processes responsible for monitoring, evaluating, and modifying emotional regulation to accomplish one's goals. Thompson (1999)

The components of emotional regulation include regulating emotions, perception and cognition, and regulating behavior (coping emotionally, cognitively, and behaviorally, p. 151 – same book). It is important we have access to a full range of emotions, can shift between emotions, confirm to cultural display rules, integrate mixed emotion, and learn to manage our emotional world. (p. 168-169)

I knew in therapy how important it was to create a therapeutic alliance where one's self-at-best can work through losses in a safe and affect-friendly environment. Emotional work is risky, unless we feel safe enough in doing deep, intensive, and extensive work. The withdrawal as a result of a traumatic experience is a normal response to the overwhelming emotions.

How could I translate this out for myself? What I needed was to balance my aloneness with socialization. In grief work, family and friends support the mourner until the working process can be endured. Those whose grief is too intense or lack a perceived support system seek outside treatment. It is a long journey to be able to live with the loss and continue to invest in life. It is the initial surviving, and examining what has and is happening that is necessary for integrating the loss into one's tapestry. Thus, unresolved trauma impairs the integration to achieve complexity to live fully by self-disregulation and emotional disequilibrium. Learning how to handle sadness, anger, and emotional pain requires identifying the root causes and underlying fears and anxieties that imprison us. To be able to feel love, joy, compassion and be emotionally accessible for a new relationship would reflect healthy reconciliation of the divorce experience.

To offer a new narrative of hope seemed like a far off possibility during my early painful days. I had to set the goal without too much contemplation. Trusting again was more about trusting myself. I felt like opening a rent-a-husband agency with a one-year lease. You wouldn't expect contentment, bliss, intimacy, or a life-long partnership. Or, would you?

A real "self" develops from childhood with a capacity to soothe itself and accept losses. This chapter bridged the earlier reactive survival emotional period to the more cognitive examination time. I know at times I've repeated myself and have elaborated on the suffering experienced. Perhaps it is not only important you understand my inability to make it just go away, but accept your own sorrowful journey until you are ready to move on. I pause to remember James Kavanaugh's poem:

Come tell me of your secret fears; where the beach is soft

as snow; where the sparkling spray binds the eyes of day;

and only I will know

There was none to share those very private thoughts that felt like weakness. Nevertheless, I was bored with myself. It was time to move on.

Striving
Self-Searching

Before I moved on to examine how the marriage failed, I needed to take stock of my failure to act. I had confused two parallel lives with one king size bed as healthy. The television occupied only one corner of the room, but it had all my husband's evening attention. If I add the sporting events to the mix, I was probably less than the exciting Super Bowl commercials.

Forget couples' therapy! Once a hidden hand and new love occupy center stage, a hardened heart usually just goes through the motions with no motivation to fix the problems. So all my hope was misplaced. There would be no undoing of his decision. I wasted the next few months in false hope. It isn't the affair that is the problem. It is the willingness to end it and not work on the marriage.

Differentiation—with integrity occurs on a spiritual level according to Wade Laquet, author of Short-Term Couples' Therapy. We spend a lifetime in and out of relationships and no time preparing for them! The goal is to pick partners who understand us and can maintain a sense of self. Each partner is often operating from an unrealistic position of how the other ought to be. So, for myself, I'm placing as the number one lesson differentiation with integrity: two separate selves capable of functioning alone and as a couple in healthy ways that work for that particular relationship.

This obviously would require some understanding of each others past needs and how it impacts the coupleship.

He was over-idealizing when we first met, I was aware of this information and his difficulty making a commitment. I ignored this knowledge, minimizing its possible significance. Now, I reflect on how it may have played a role in his disenchantment.

Imago theory suggests we've turned off our feelings or thinking during childhood and marry someone to complete our poor socialization. Actually, we would do well to develop that part of our self, but often we become triggered by a partner. We can become angry when romantic love wanes as it usually does, thinking it is an end to itself. By defending against the loss of romantic love, we are responding to normal frustrations that are trying to alert us to a need for growth.

Wounds are created during the developmental process and trying to restore the functions of ourselves lost in socialization, we doom ourselves to pick partners similar to one another and to one of our parents. Those who work with couples in the Imago tradition; see relationship ruptures, not individuals as the focus. The main tenet is that each person is a creation and function of relationship and in turn is a creator of the relationship in which they function. (Wade Luquet in Short-Term Couples Therapy.)

My professional work with couples has been to work both individually and as a couple. Marriages are mostly created and maintained on an unconscious level. By helping to bring automatic behaviors into self-awareness, examining underlying rationale and addressing assumptions each can modify positions. The word script can be used to include the following six areas for work: sex, communication, romance, identity, personality and trust.

I could see the need to work back through my earlier losses and how I surrendered pieces of myself. Why was that so significant? It was reasonable to assume perhaps Imago theory was right: "Nature had put together myself and my partners who were injured at the same place developmentally and missing opposite parts of themselves in an effort to get their developmental needs met and to regain lost parts of themselves. Nor surprisingly, most of us don't know this secret and rather than cooperating with nature, we re-injure our partners in our effort to defend ourselves. For us to heal in our relationships, we must grasp the concept that nature is using relationships to help us regain our wholeness. The trick is for us to cooperate with nature".

Imago begins with the idea a couple has to be committed to do the healing work. That took out my husband. He had another engagement.

I won't be able to figure out why he left, but I can examine how blinded I was to the quality of the relationship.

Perhaps I couldn't own a failure and had to maintain the illusion. On the other hand, when your needs are being met in many ways, you are not as likely to look just to a partner for all your needs. I felt safe and had little known frustrations. How quickly that can change! I couldn't make sense by analyzing the hit. I moved to the trauma that resulted.

CHAPTER 6
EXAMINING

This chapter addresses the denial we generally experience during the initial onslaught, preferring to hide from the painful truth that it's really over. More often, we come to realize only piecemeal the depth and breadth of the terminated coupleship. We'll explore defense mechanisms and how they respond to a lifetime of patterning. Sometimes they protect us from the harsh cruelty of loss by concealing past, present, and future ramifications. Adaptive denial, as we shall see, can be helpful in the beginning to assist us in adjusting to our unexpected condition. We begin to recognize our need to move from victim to survivor to life-participant and how this progression can be accomplished. You will see my progression in my "best self "as an example of the inner work that was ongoing from the start and continues today.

I waffled and wavered on where I was and what my destination was going to be. Fearful and tearful, I had managed to subsist in the survival period. I was now ready to delve into anything that would provide answers. Unfortunately, the self-examination process is more an exploratory art form than an absolute science. I kept opening up anything that might provide enlightenment. I wanted desperately to understand why and how this happened, although I already knew it would make no difference in the outcome. Nevertheless, I was perplexed and obsessed with pondering all the whys.

Denial

Denial is a reaction to unwanted or unacceptable thoughts and feelings. Usually, denial helps us in the short term to maintain a sense of security, however false. We also avoid feelings of shame and guilt. Unconsciously, we hide information from our consciousness, somehow saying "no" to unwanted parts of reality. We can deny only parts of the story -significance of the loss is probably the most commonly seen in therapy. We may have no awareness for years that we've chosen not to face certain truths. I know now I was covering up for a long time something that was rotten in paradise until my paradise was tossed.

Significantly, the desire to avoid disrupting a relationship is the most important and powerful motive for denying feelings. Marital conflict can trigger earlier fears of rejection, abandonment, guilt, or shame. You probably know how it goes: Conversations stay on safe topics. There is an unspoken distorted view of reality, in which the intimate problems go unidentified, unadmitted, and therefore unresolved. There are smiles and murmurs and too many "Yes, dears," for years.

But the act of thwarting efforts to admit, diagnose, and solve problems in a relationship uses more energy to sustain the self-deception than to preserve the status quo. While the partner in denial may get his or her needs met, the other may not. Clearly, very often in therapy, I see long-term relationships being over-idealized and problems denied by the spouse that has been left. This over-idealization promotes false hope and more grief.

One of the most important aspects is to examine the marital relationship and identify points of change and complicity. Perhaps the early signs were overlooked. Perhaps later signals were denied. Perhaps too much was swept under the rug, or behind the TV, for too long.

Initially, the sorrow of being abandoned may be overshadowed by the need to idealize the spouse who has moved on. Making the person into either a king or scoundrel is unhealthy. Assessing the relationship and the use of self-reflection may provide understanding, self-awareness from lessons, and future changes.

This self-reflection, "examining", is the best defense against future patterning, that is, picking the same type of individual or the opposite and adopting a similar pattern. Our denial can be somewhat protective, and slowly we begin to discover and own the truth about ourselves and our now "insignificant other." Forgiveness will be hard-won, only by surrendering our mean-spiritedness and invoking a generosity we may not feel at first, will our peace be regained and our energy released to freely flourish. I will begin here with a self-examination.

Regardless of how painful the process, I needed desperately to make sense of the separation, or rather the marriage and my responses to the divorce. They call it Monday night quarterbacking to do the "shoulds" and "coulds", after the game is lost. If I just up and blamed my husband for everything, I was destined to live smugly, dishonestly, and without the changes from lessons learned. <u>The Partner</u> would heal all those childhood wounds and accept all my psychopathology resulting from earlier losses.

Somehow this person would read my mind and fulfill all my longings. The list could be made ad nauseam. I wasn't the one with the complaints so therefore I was the perfect partner who endured the other's idiosyncrasies. Does that sound familiar? Let me share what I know concerning the fit between partners, the co-creation of the relationship, and frequent areas of disagreement.

I've always subscribed to some of the work Jung and Holland did on the unconscious and personality types. "Vast stores of images, relationships, patterns, symbols, and archetypes that sway our behavior and body language, shape our dreams, bind our families and communities together, and give a sense of meaning to our lives without reference to rational thought. This is the part of the self where skills and patterns are embedded in our bodies and in the neutral networks of the brain". SQ – Spiritual Intelligence (the ultimate intelligence). Danah Zohar & Dr. Ian Marshall – (2000) Bloomsbury Pub., St. Martin's, NY & London Press, p. 136.

So there is some biology that limits our ability to freely choose all that we want to be (more of a rational choice). My husband was clearly very different from myself. I was attractive for him initially. I had a tremendous need to replay that tragic August night and begin editing and reframing what I would come to believe. My marriage was good enoughI'm pretty sure that was the case until someone took aim for my husband's heart. She worked with him, knew he was married, and laid claim to him anyway. Of course, he was 100% responsible for his infidelity, lies, and betrayal. He may have blown up the marriage unilaterally, but I admit he had to have been dissatisfied or less satisfied than he portrayed. I know now my hope he would return influenced making his new love the target for all my suffering. She scooted in, and I slithered out. She had a ready made life, one I relished and was grateful for. As we exchanged titles, I watched in horror as my life crumbled. I allowed myself to empty. I was in a serious loss. By the end of this first nine months, I recognized my nesting was narcisstic and rendering me devoid of motivation. I became entrenched in my safe office that had the potential for avoidance. Oh, I looked productive; however I was shutting out the truth. I was going to be divorced from a man who no longer loved me or wanted to cohabitate.

He was so miserable he was willing to destroy our friendship. My sins were those of omission—much harder to recognize and take responsibility for. The survival period was a mix of present, past, and future losses and fears. I had surrendered significant pieces of autonomy during the marriage. My conceptualization was shifting as I used a more insightful approach, as I'm very visual. I drew a series of apothecary jars to represent myself in the relationship. I saw the past occupying an insignificant impact on present circumstances. The future with my husband was positive—sealed in concrete. I was happily married, felt good about myself, and had no thoughts of the storm that was brewing. I couldn't believe the news our marriage was over and totally blamed his girlfriend.

At one point my husband admitted if not for this relationship he would have stayed. He failed to say he loved me and wanted our relationship to thrive. It took a great deal of self-examination to realize it wasn't about his girlfriend. He was clearly no longer committed. In time someone would have come along. There was no sex and no affection. What part of this was I not getting?

In Flannery, J.R. Survival Work from Victim... p. 217 in Van der Kolk (1987), he uses the stress management approach to treat learned helplessness and emphasizes the need for gaining a sense of mastery. A good social support network may help, coupled with a good pre-morbid level of coping skills. Stress-resistant individuals have control and involvement operating in their lives. Their stabilized daily routine and ability to seek out social support when faced with adversity foster a belief that their actions will help them resolve their problems. This results in a general mood of wellbeing or at least hopefulness about the future.

Solomon, M. & Siegel, D. Healing Trauma (2003) describe a person who is likely to fail to integrate the trauma into the totality of his or her life experiences:

"Individuals who lack contingency between response and outcomesin painful situations from which there is no escape, who hold themselves personally responsible, when in fact nothing can be done, who perceive the problem to be long lived, and who believe the inability to function will be wide-spread would be most likely to have performance decrements and depressed mood." (p. 43, 44)

If the anxiety and fear of making the list were high, I could only imagine the cost of denial. Only by owning my feelings could I begin to address them and find new ways to meet my goals. Anger would serve to block any progress. Creativity retreats when all my energy is directed towards the behaviors of someone else. I could not undo what happened. I had poured into my marriage to the best of my ability. I needed to pour into myself! I was ashamed of my interdependency and yet that had been a healthy choice for me.

Human needs are programmed to be met, in part, by other humans. Activities, music, computers, books, and television may satisfy for a time but are not perfect substitutes for community involvement. Pets provide love and companionship but little risk. Initially, taking risks to love again and trust others may be a lofty goal. Blaming others for our circumstances and remaining in a nonfunctional state are forms of denial. Overanalyzing the situation but failing to make change and fashion our lives is to make ourselves prisoners of our own inaction.

My denial was at first a profound refusal to recognize my position: hopeless as far as my marriage was concerned. Denial is such a powerful unconscious defense mechanism. It sheltered me initially from my painful state. As I accepted the reality, my choices became unlimited regarding myself, but not in saving a marriage that had been assassinated by my spouse.

My friends Sandie and Gale kept telling me I needed an attorney. Their disbelief at my stubbornness in thinking he would come to his senses was only exceeded by my belief he still loved me. He kept telling me so: "I love you but I just don't want to be married to you." We all know about this kind of "but." Translated it really means: MOVE ON! The cowards refuse to accept your withdrawal and will play out the I-love-you like a melodrama until their purposes are revealed.

I refused to listen to anyone. He told me his attorney friend advised him to serve the divorce papers. My belief in the tooth fairy was about as realistic as my thinking was. I hadn't received the papers and, until I did, my skewed thinking told me, there was still a chance. But it wouldn't be long before I was served—to my profound shock.

Adaptive denial is present when you try to spare yourself a painful state by feeding yourself small droplets of the horrible reality over time so you can finally accept it. Thank goodness my friends continued to badger me until I came to my senses and employed an attorney.

The antithesis of denial would be achieving a sense of empowerment in areas that formerly left you feeling helpless and traumatized, such as accepting losses, working through them, and moving on. Instead of self-protection from the painful thoughts, you would learn to process them without being overwhelmed or letting them take over your life, such as the sense of feeling abandoned and betrayed.

Melody Beattie's meditation book <u>The Language of Letting Go</u> is about releasing control that is impossible to successfully impose on self and others. My favorite I want to share with you:

Going with the Flow

"Go with the Flow. Let go of fear and your need to control. Relinquish anxiety. Let it slip away, as you dive into the river of the present moment, the river of your life, your place in the universe.

Stop trying to force the direction. Try not to swim against the current, unless it is necessary for your survival. If you've been clinging to a branch at the riverside, let go.

Let yourself move forward. Let yourself be moved forward.

Avoid the rapids when possible. If you can't, stay relaxed. Staying relaxed can take you safely through fierce currents. If you go under for a moment, allow yourself to surface naturally. You will.

Appreciate the beauty of the scenery, as it is. See things with freshness, with newness. You shall never pass by today's scenery again!

Don't think too hard about things. The flow is meant to be experienced. Within it, care for yourself. You are part of the flow, an important part. Work with the flow. Work within the flow. Thrashing about isn't necessary. Let the flow help you care for yourself. Let it help you set boundaries, make decisions, and get you where you need to be when it is time.

"You can trust the flow, and your part in it.

Today, I will go with the flow."

Beattie, M. (1990) p.191, Language of Letting Go.

I fought the current relentlessly, truly believing I could overcome the undertow. It wore me out! I know now there is a time to hold up, fold up, walk away, and run (Kenny Rogers in *The Gambler*). It is the fear and anxiety that drives us to restlessness and irritability, almost unbearable for joyful individuals to relax and let go.

Letting go of a love constricts our world and places us in victim modality. Not only has this love been removed, but unless we embrace our new lives, we pass up all the present and future love from others in our lives. My own unreasonable expectations blocked out any other options for I refused to let go of an emotionally unavailable man. I never jockeyed for a control position. I couldn't live up to my partner's standards and exaggerated expectations of who I was. I had to let go that someone else was going to rescue me from the dread. To love is a choice.

Being victimized in a lost relationship and failing to take responsibility to move forward is a self-secondary victimization. Avoidance of working through the intense emotional experience only leads to a toxic denial of feelings. Anger tends to surface and keeps true connections with others from happening.

Enmeshing myself in the circumstances surrounding an event was hardly a choice initially. Now it is. I can refocus myself with self-talk to let go of what I cannot change. I can refuse to become a workaholic to keep feeling valueless. It isn't about my accomplishments, but rather the loss of my personal self.

Others may fight the weariness of a meaningless existence without a partner they were devoted to.

Self worth will not be found in external environments. It is the inner work that frees us from both the lack of investing in our environments and the over-investing. The bored actually are pouring attention into avoiding anything outside themselves.

Authentic power is about dealing with pain, sorrow, and fears of yesterday and seeming laid back can appear as indifference. Questioning by a partner can be perceived as intrusive and demanding. Thus, what works in the beginning becomes annoying. With a relationship breakup, each can feel self-righteous. Laid back is often a way of avoiding the intimacy and conflicts. Individual attachment styles do not go away but can be modified by changing responses. The behaviors each of us adapts in coupleships make us feel comfort and safety. Unfortunately, the present style quite often resembles the infant, only now there are two jockeying for position.

The ability to honor a partner's need for solitude or silence without being threatened comes from a secure childhood. In <u>Couple Fits</u> Cohen & Roqouin reflect on secure individuals as having no fear of confrontation, able to offer forgiveness, capable of seeing two sides to a story, and able to discover options. They can be in danger of missing the fun in life because of always doing what is right. They also exhibit the ability to be trust worthy but somewhat naïve about others. It may be difficult for them to take honest stock of others and let go of poor choices.

Growth would represent better more honest communication when annoyed, not engaging in hero worship, showing ongoing appreciation, accept genuine complaints, and increase awareness of all the positive aspects.

Letting-go means relinquishing feelings of being vulnerable. Owning my feelings can lend to not allowing them to control my behavior. The other side is permitting the good feelings of love, peace, joy, and happiness to exist.

Do I know I can often remove myself from victim roles? Denial is a powerful shock absorber until I am ready to face the issue.

Additionally, not feeling the need to use an addiction to insulate yourself from the pain would be a sign of reality acceptance. Our "urge to merge" causes us to block off our feelings of pain, rage, and fear. We sometimes make a pursuit of closeness a life theme in an effort to assuage the anxiety of separateness. We invest our lovers and partners with high expectations of being all-encompassing nurturing beings. When they reject us, we feel as though we are pierced through the heart, as it destroys the longing for oneness. This trauma so impacts our coping mechanisms that denial prevails, accompanied by the strong false hope that magically things will return to the original place and situation and feelings.

From Survivor to Life-Participant: Admitting What We Need To

From these observations and others, four stress-resistant coping strategies increase adaptation in response to adverse situations:

1. Taking personal control.
2. Becoming task-oriented.
3. Making healthful life changes.
4. Utilizing social supports.

We must also face what the loss will bring us, in emotional and economic costs. I struggled to own the costs of the divorce:

- Initially, a loss of self-assurance.
- Knowledge I would grow older alone.
- Surrendering the comfort, communication, and chemistry my relationship provided.
- The thought of going off into the sunset not hand-in-hand but in a solitary mode, holding my own hand.
- Assuming full economic responsibility for myself without a backup plan.

Healing our personal narratives, examining our original sense of abandonment and betrayal and the events that followed, helps us formulate new pathways with a more complete and renewed sense of self. First we need to examine where we came from. This takes time, tools, and a commitment to work towards a new beginning.

I could try to pretend all the pain is gone and focus on all the healing. But now, it's not the rejection and betrayal that hurt so much—I've worked through these. Instead, it's the feeling of failure that somehow I have not been what I needed to be, although I still don't know what that is. This is what plagues me.

It is authentic to own the losses, trust my heart and head and all who I was, who I am, and ever could be. I still harbor negative feelings but want to avoid feeling jealous, angry, and possessive, and silence the attachment-hungry me. Instead, I've have admitted how bad I felt. I've soothed and bathed myself in spiritual love. By letting go of my need for perfection, I can examine where I've been and where I want to go. This is the place I am at this stage. The next stage is equally necessary and difficult for me and others to engage. By recording the traumatic event and our self-discoveries, we can begin to hear our own moaning and groaning leading to growth.

DOCUMENTING

Documentation of our Lewis & Clark journey can help serve the feedback loop to the brain etching in a revision of what happened, working through, and healing. Each time we overcome a traumatic event, there exists opportunities for adding to life's coping toolbox. We can draw on our discoveries for ourselves and to help others.

Healing in Community

Once in a while a group of whales will lose their sense of direction and head for shore. It is believed that whales and dolphins beach themselves along Florida's coastline due to parasite infestation.

Groups of animal lovers turn out to help herd the lost whales in the shallows until they can return to the open waters. Hands are laid on the whales, and they are soothed by human contact. At some point, the whales must return to the deeper waters on their own.

Each of us must survive the shallows...that time in our lives when we feel abandoned and deserted. We have to make a determination to reach out for help, other human contact, or remain stuck, beached, in our sorrow. Moving into deeper waters means taking risk again. Family and friends are bewildered by losses and have great difficulty meeting unmet needs unless we can identify them and help ourselves stay afloat and move forward as we are capable of doing so. All the self-help materials and groups are tools to help us take action. Remember, our trauma is a rupture in a relationship bond.

Self-reflection and a full acceptance of mourning your losses is a sound plan of action for surviving the survival phase. Your journal/scrapbook can help you identify your thoughts and feelings so you understand the significance of your losses. You'll be ready to move into a more global examination of what happened and where to go from here in time.

Avoid addictions that will be difficult to surrender, such as to foods, drink, shopping, and the like. Do try to eat healthy foods and exercise daily. This will help you sleep and face your problems squarely

The Appendices

I have included a collection of self-help materials in Appendix A which consists of check sheets for self-assessments. Appendix B, a very involved look at the different roles one plays utilizing a creative approach.

Utilize the assessment and exercises in Appendix A and B. As I did, and continue to do so, use the maxims in Appendix C for inspiration. .

Only you can determine where you are in the process and your readiness to move forward. Now that you may feel a little desire to live more fully, you can reeducate yourself concerning your emotions.

<u>REMEMBER...THIS TOO SHALL PASS. REFUSE TO TRAVEL INTO THE FUTURE AND MAKE IT INTO A HOPELESS JOURNEY.</u> Monitor both the self-regulation and emotional control at this more active time. Documenting how you are working on self-regulation and gaining emotional control processing is essential. In Solomon and Siegel, <u>Healing Trauma</u>, (2003) observe, for "adaptive flexibility of the mind to respond to changes in the internal and external environments. Tolerance for change and the ability to increase capacity for dealing with a wider range and intensity of emotion would occur." (p. 53). If we fail to process what has happened—either by unconsciously avoiding or intrusively flooding ourselves—we can become disabled (assuming one is not in a therapeutic setting).

Eight Steps to Self-Examination and Documenting

Initially, I wrote the prologue and kept progress notes on my pilgrimage. I wasn't keeping a daily record but more spontaneous notes. I outlined well over fifty books and began reconstructing an emotional primer. I probably have enough materials to write another six books. I slowly began challenging and replacing faulty thinking with a more sensible account. I travel back and forth into my anecdotal pieces and continue to edit out old thinking for the new and revised version. I'm listing what worked and works for me in the next eight steps.

First, identify various feelings, thoughts, and behaviors that are plaguing your ability to feel whole. (See the questions and check sheets in Appendix A; they helped me tremendously.)

Second, formulate a plan as to how you can begin to tease apart your tapestry and release the non-productive, energy-draining negative emotions that are no longer serving you. Once you know what is happening, it takes problem solving steps to remove the road blocks. Third, move to collecting your writing, art, poems into a journal, scrapbook, or computer file. Record your narrative, revisions, progress and setbacks.

Fourth, as you begin your new journey, put "stops" in place to remind you of your new learning "stops".

S.T.O.P.S. stands for sticking to owning personal scripts—not someone else's. Just because someone else called you a name or labeled you does not make it your truth. Clearly, challenge notes you disagree with but want to journal. Write with a discerning mind.

Fifth, create a team of support people and activities to replace negative "friends" and habits. Know where to go for a particular problem.

Sixth, create a bibliography of books you would like to include in your learning library. Hit the library, friends, book sales, and garage sales. Second-hand book stores work! Use the exercises in Part IV, Appendix B, to set up your doors and sub-personality chart. The door exercise asks you to create a wall of doors to tuck each separate traumatic event or loss behind. Instead of being flooded by the sum total of events, each one can be addressed separately and closed until another time.

The sub-personality exercise teases apart different parts of us that operate in a variety of roles. Charts are created to help identify goals and ways sub-personalities respond in crisis. By understanding ourselves, we can better work on various roles we play.

Seventh, continue to examine your ongoing present thoughts for signs that you are renting space in your head for past anger and resentment. Evict them! We are spiritual beings and have skills and a foundation to aid our recovery.

Eighth, talk to God. Share your plan and pray for guidance. Talk to individuals you respect and admire whose lives have evidenced trauma yet who are now living fully on their path. Seek help from spiritual materials and include learning in your plan.

Growth requires an honest inventory of strengths and weaknesses. Knowing ourselves is not about judgment. It is an assessment examination of all of our losses so we can engage in a working-through process and a psychological and emotional makeover. Our core self remains fairly constant and works well with truth, not self-deception.

To summarize, now you have:

1. The areas you need to address.
2. Books that address them.
3. Some manner of recording, diagramming, expressing your thoughts and feelings on paper. Poems, stories, pictures, even songs and videos all work.
4. A door chart with those areas/items that flood you.
5. A sub-personality chart to see what part of you is sabotaging all of you.

Set small journeys: ask that saboteur personality to identify perceived causes for the anger. Develop a plan for letting go. Begin following advice in self-help journals and in this book. Practice releasing the problems as they are resolved. There is no completion of a process model. As you learn and grow, you remodel those areas you want to address.

Your next mission will be to begin to let go of past hurts through forgiveness and inch forward. Chart your progress. You've survived the hit, your heart seemed broken, however, you've taken responsibility for your healing. Who else knows you and can direct your inner journey? It will be a process of re-experiencing, surviving, examining, letting go, and fashioning a new life.

It is time to remember the pen is mightier than the sword or tear-stained pillow. Part IV, Appendixes A, B, and C, are meant to help you create a written foundation. Document your learning and progress. Do what you need and want to in your own way. When you are satisfied with your documenting, continue reading here. You will then be ready for Chapters 7 and 8, letting go and fashioning a new life.

CHAPTER 7

LETTING GO

Lessons come from the simplest pleasures. Collecting shells, watching children build sand castles, and walking the beach do not require rocket scientist thinking. I see only the beauty when I am in that frame of mind, ignoring the coastal destruction that can occur.

In Florida, wherever you are, there is probably a beach no more than a gas tank away. No geographical point is more than 60 miles from salt water. All of my memories of Palm Island revolve around those two miles of picturesque beach, teeming with the real Floridian natives...turtles, pelicans, and laughing gulls. I love the mounds of shells, many of which have traveled from Caribbean and Gulf waters, transported by strong tides and currents. I wade out into the surf line where the breaking waves mash collectible shells. I take only a few of each, respectful of my find, and never pick up one occupied by a living creature without tossing it back into the ocean.

I have constructed an imaginary bridge built with visual and olfactory stimuli to channel my stress. My office entryway has a colorful potpourri garden filled with shells. Children and adults alike take home shell souvenirs. My cell phone opens to a photo of my coffee table centerpiece, shells surrounding a seashell scented candle. My memories and linking objects transport me to a relaxing beach where I am free to surrender the stress of the moment.

Probably the most important lesson I have learned to date is the one and only person I have any control over is myself. Believing that tenet and operating first as a self and second as a self in relationship helps me continue to let go of any fantasy. I can ensure my own survival by feeding myself and not someone else. Even the airlines tell you to don your oxygen mask before putting one on a child. Letting-go of irrational thinking frees me to care for myself and others in non-controlling ways. I can make requests and even demands, but there is no spouse-owner policy.

Sand Castles of Yesterday

I remember as a child constructing elaborate sand castles surrounded by moats to channel the water away from my creation. Contests in some coastal towns challenge local castle artists to create magnificent sculptures. The impermanence of the beach, at the mercy of all of nature, is the perfect setting for art to be enjoyed, remembered, and surrendered. Washed away—a most meaningful expression for change—accepting what I can and cannot hold on to…..letting go…..making room for new friends, goals, and experiences.

I readily identify with the island palms that bend without breaking. I thought of their uprooting during Hurricane Andrew and successful replanting. Shored up with scrap wood and nails, they could be replanted and take root again. Several varieties contort themselves to adapt to the circumstances of their environment.

Changing our Thinking

Marriages need to be flexible with a strong root system. Families, friends, and the culture contribute positive and negative elements that reflect resiliency. An unwanted divorce (and even a "wanted one") not only affects the present but can paralyze our potentials if we permit it. I want on-going reality checks….every so many miles.

Some traumatic events become the starting point for lives of meaningful service. Healing is not a given. It is won on the battleground of broken promises, unmet expectations, and shattered dreams. It requires infinite patience, healthy self-esteem, a good support system, and the ability to deal with ambivalence.

Let's examine some of the ways we can equip ourselves for the tasks at hand, especially letting go.

What if we actually recognized that marriages in these incredible, highly communicative times are unlikely to provide all the cultural expectations and fantasy fulfillment promoted by the culture? I'd like to offer a course for young adults in college, maybe as early as 11th and 12th grades. I'd call it "Shattered Dreams," to counteract the Cinderella fantasies and prepare them for what marriage and true partnership really are.

Healthy self-development and self-esteem, plus corrective experiences when necessary, would insure resiliency and the ability to have an intimate relationship.

If we prepare young people to do as good a job matchmaking as they do in all their other pursuits, we might begin to address depressions and anxieties that begin in these times and head off much misery later.

Addictive or Additive Relationships

Most of the problems of letting go center around the addictive nature of relationships. Somehow these relationships become a "compulsive component" that keeps us from re-experiencing frightening feelings of childhood. By stepping out from the abandonment place as "the victim," facing our fears, owning our compulsions and addictions, we begin to liberate ourselves from the torment.

If a partner is essential to mirror who we are, this means our image disappears with them if they leave. In this frame, to lose a partner is to lose ourselves. Of course, the tendency is to find another person who fulfills our needs in the same way and do the same thing. But by such moves, we neglect making ourselves whole. Emptiness is not about the other disappearing. It is about myself temporarily lost due to the loss. Others offer us an illusion of safety. Unless we let go of the myth that the two of us are one and neither will ever leave, our anxiety remains under the surface like a submerged iceberg, threatening to emerge at the slightest tremor in the relationship. The prescription that being with the other is a matter of life and death is self-destructive. We may replay this futile drama for years instead of engaging in self-exploration, letting go of a dead relationship, and investing our love elsewhere. Letting go of love for the unresponsive other and remodeling our inner world can begin a new development of our inner security.

When your attachment needs are dominant and running your life, you may oscillate between love and hate, as if the other person is two people. Distrust in the form of jealousy or an obsession will engulf you. Jealousy is more about overvaluing your partner over yourself than loving them. Such feelings originate with our mothers and the exclusive relationship we once had with them. We surrender our personal power and often struggle with a chronic fantasy of leaving. It takes a real problem- solving approach to recognize how legitimate our accusations really are. Addictive relationships contain less love and respect and more hostility, anger, and anxiety. Peace comes from recognizing our options and addressing concerns in a positive way. By accepting your partner's complexity and giving up the ability to change a departing spouse's mind, you free yourself. In my case, there were no closures from any productive discussions. I had to do my solo work post divorce.

I recognize now how fantasy had always played a rather large role in my life. It provided a place of comfort in imagination and camouflaged severe flaws in my relationship. It was a major element in my being so shocked and hopeful for so long. I wasn't the perfect partner, but I also wasn't the most imperfect partner. My real self has been quite capable of dealing with the reality that he no longer loved me or wanted to share his life with me. Despite the intense pain of this declaration, I've not engaged in self-destructive behavior. Through all the means chronicled and suggested here, I've learned to let go and fashion a new life for myself. It has been a tremendous challenge and will at times continue to be a part of a disappointment. Myself at times wants what it lost. I soothe and remind myself it only lost what it thought it had. It is more likely it had and lost a little, but gave up much of itself in the process. But now, having survived the divorce and gone through many previous tasks of survival, grief, and mourning, it is the fashioning of my life from here where I invest my energy. Examining and letting go are ongoing processes, but they now take place in the context of refashioning.

CHAPTER 8

FASHIONING

On one of the first visits to Palm Island, our friends took us on a field trip down the Peace River. Playful manatees, struggling to survive boats and barge collisions, inhabit Florida's waters. They have no natural enemies in the wild—not even sharks or alligators. Manatee females give birth in their seventh to ninth year, keeping their calves nearby for two years or more.

They are fairly docile vegetarians who are neither territorial nor aggressive. They do form groups and play together, but these associations are usually temporary. The manatee is essentially a solitary animal, Kadell, J., 1992 "Manatee" in the Florida Survival Handbook, Costal Printing, Inc., Sarasota, FL.

Initially, somewhat like the manatee, we are both solitary and social. We hide by pulling into ourselves. We're afraid to almost move because the pain is so intense. Not only do we try to protect ourselves but to spare others who would be sad with and around us. We also try to make sense of our experiences that do not fit with our view of the world. We tend to come up with plausible explanations for why such horrible things have happened to us.

We may see the world as a cruel and unforgiving place. We probably felt we were powerless and victimized. If we don't challenge these world views, we may simply continue to act in accordance with them. Silence, lack of self-examination, and ignorance of our thoughts and feelings cause us to refuse to take risks by not reinvesting in life.

There is not a magical line of demarcation where surviving ends and striving begins. Grief comes and goes like the waves. Human complexity allows us to have many competing thoughts and feelings as we travel on our journey. Acceptance of our inability to have total control is a surrendering that makes room for new thinking, feeling, and behaving.

By not glossing over the event or maintaining silence, we prompt our ability to personally come to terms with all we've lost, to work through it, let go, and fashion a new pathway. By containing ourselves from the urge to chuck out all reminders, we can learn to enjoy memories and memorabilia from our marriage without painful aftermath, just as with death. Children of divorce profit from our taking the higher road of forgiveness and moving on. It isn't the divorce that creates and wreaks as much havoc; as our inability to forgive and establish a co-parenting relationship.

Hanging On

Even after all my work on myself, it was difficult not to pick up the phone and call my ex-husband when I was hurting. He had been my best friend for years, long before we married. But of course, he was the reason I was so sad.

Post-breakups create chaotic environments of hanging on—one still calls, begs, drops by, sleeps with a spouse soon to be ex-ed out. You begin day one of dealing with the separation anxiety and abandonment by trying to win someone back in this manner. Even crawling back to the rejecter is suspect of a temporary solution, unless accompanied by some type of couple communication or therapy. Otherwise, you'll be vulnerable for further abandonment.

I didn't have to worry about being seduced sexually during the "great divide". He wasn't interested before, during, or post marriage. Sexless, passionless marriages often have an angry, hostile underpinning. More often than not, one partner bangs his/her head against a wall trying to manipulate the other into having sex. Making love is usually reserved for better relationships. Uncoupling begins as a quiet unilateral process (Splitting Up, p.63).

Outwardly, the rejecter continues to look like part of a couple. Inwardly, a private, separate world has been formed and resentment grows toward the jailer. The cost may be high: moral integrity, peace of mind, and attention to duties. (Splitting Up, p.63). Additionally, by not recognizing the infidelity, the cheating partner builds a case excusing behavior due to the lack of interest the mate is showing. (Splitting Up, p. 71).

Much of mankind's sufferings arrive not from loving but from infantile demands for love in some form…..too strong needs to be loved may conflict with our cultural standards of self-reliant individualism so that injured self-esteem generates intense and unremitting rage out of feelings of inferiority. Rage is engendered by failure to satisfy excessive needs to be loved which are predestined to failure because the adult cannot satisfy needs which belong to childhood. Therapy or controlled dating would probably provide more information and lead to less suffering, in determining whether the relationship can resume.

A great little book if you're still experiencing an inordinate amount of ex-residue is Kuster's *Exorcising Your Ex* (1996). An important point Kuster makes, even if we don't want to face it, is that the reason exes are exes is they are wrong for you, even if they initiated the breakup. We must unload the baggage if we are to move on and explore the possibility of a new relationship.

Baggage has traveled the journey post separation as with a death. Physical separation does not necessarily end the emotional ties. My autobiographical self carried words and full paragraphs of rejection from the first minutes on. Who ever said "sticks and stones may break our bones but names will never hurt me" must have been in a coma. Letting go took conscious effort and a goal of not repeating them to myself or others. (Surviving Infidelity, Subotnik & Morris (2005) is an excellent self-help book to bring closure).

Painful memories revolved around places, music, television, and relationships. I relinquished those things that were going to trigger discomfort and interfere with my journey. Things were packed away until I could reflect on whether I wanted or needed to include them in my life. Learning how to focus on the whole of the relationship involves letting go of the baggage and moving forward. I've always felt things could be best dealt with when I had control. Now I know I need less control, more letting go, and making room for a new relationship.

I also had to remove the discarded dreams, the main one being authoring books and growing old with my husband on Palm Island. That kind of baggage is highly resistant to any type of exchange program.

So painful memories triggered by memorabilia, material reminders, and drive bys all add weight to our emotional cauldron. Letting go frees us and makes room for the universe to endow us with newness—the fashioning part.

When You Don't Want to Stay Single

When you don't want to stay single, you'll need to do a high volume amount of dating and the internet is promising for reaching a large audience for you to……....

Rachel Greenwald's *Find a Husband After 35* is a wonderful little book that asks "Why are you still single and what are you going to do about it?". If you absolutely do not want to live more than one hour single, this is a good place to begin. In her simple 15-step action program, she offers practical help for why online dating is a crucial activity after 35:

1. High Volume (You can reach a multitude quickly & economically.)
2. Fast (A whole list in 30 mins. if you are lucky.)
3. Inexpensive (Just pennies compared to going out.)
4. Convenient (Whenever the spirit moves you.)
5. What Counts (You may screen for looks, activities, income. You may be fooled.)
6. Better Ratio (Not everyone is computer hunting.)
7. Anonymous (No one really has access to your world. Initially, safer.)

Of course, one of the biggest risks you might take is that you could be talking to a 14-year-old on line without knowing it!

I would not suggest registering on dating sites until you've been able to address your role in the relationship, work through the lifestyle changes, and live independently. If you are too needy, you may distance yourself more socially and further withdraw by being attracted to emotionally unavailable individuals. Greenwald offers multiple marketing tips for finding mates and dates.

Therapy and Self-Therapy: A Process of Heartwork:

My first nine months birthed a wounded wimp. The next year I became more alive and angry. All my research and writing helped me with my AMA experience that I was fully present in the marriage and divorce. My advice is to get healthy before recoupling. This would include:

1. Excavating the broken parts
2. Debriefing the shame, guilt, blame and negativity
3. Owning feelings, thoughts, and behaviors
4. Working through the loss
5. Not isolating yourself
6. Becoming self-nourishing.
7. Reinvesting in life by embracing a community,

When I reflect on those first two years and how unfair I thought they were, I realize how much I've grown in these last four. It would be easy to say I'm responsible for my feelings—and of course I am, but in truth I've always been other-focused—a pleaser. I still am! Recognizing this, the difference is I've let go of the fear of being imperfect or rejected because I've missed the pleasing mark. And I'm pleased to say fashioning a new life and lifestyle.

Self-help books abound on fixing relationships. Just reading everything in sight will not necessarily change how you feel, think, or act. I formulated a self-help plan that included the following:

1. I set my major goals for my life space. That meant deciding what was significant—(my world, my book, my friends, my children.) How would dating or mating fit into my life rather than surrendering my life and embracing someone else's?

2. What type of individuals would be most likely to be happy sharing space with me and vice versa?

3. How could I best achieve balance and harmony in being myself and being with others?

4. Would I want to expand activities or not?

5. What areas needed ongoing shaping and how would I accomplish the goals I choose for myself?

6. I wanted to have an attitude of gratitude, not a negative one. This was a relevant safety space I wanted to create. I found a spiritual quest most comforting. Some individuals perhaps do not need to delve so deep nor work so long and hard. Whatever your pace is, however, you choose your journey and make it an ongoing process without a final destination. Ongoing assessments, learning how to soothe yourself, expanding knowledge, strengthening coping skills, improving communication, taking risks to love again are all worthy and possible areas for achievement.

I would like to review and recommend books that helped me as you begin revamping your wardrobe and refashioning your life. So many clients blame themselves for being between 25-30 years old and partnerless. I was convinced for sometime the difficulty is less personal.

The works selected are as follows:

<u>Unhooked Generation</u> by Julian Straus. She used a small sample of 100 individuals whom she interviewed in one of six cities (San Francisco, Los Angeles, Chicago, Minneapolis, Dallas, and New York). The participants were single men and women in their 20's and 30's. Her interviews focused on dating success and failures. She points out "seven evil influences" that were not operating in older generations.

1. <u>The Cult of I</u> – (A self-absorbed culture with high technology to propagate the messages<u>.)</u>
2. <u>A Multiple Choice Culture</u> – (Looks like dates are plentiful but in reality unavailable for permanent relationships.)
3. <u>The Divorce Effect</u> – (Have produced independent children who are self-nourishing and ambivalent about relationships.)
4. <u>Inadvertent Effects of Feminism</u> – (Which she supports but have alienated marriages.)
5. <u>Why Suffer Mentality</u> – (Refuse to work out and suffer anything-climb out.)
6. <u>The Celebrity Standard</u> – (Fantasy based on media give distortions about romance/love.)
7. <u>Fallout From Marriage Delays</u> – (More self-protective, less open for love.)

It was reaffirming to know her research promoted the role of cultural influences as it is of epidemic proportions many childless individuals will be so because of not having a willing, capable, partner.

<u>The Velveteen Principles: A Guide to Becoming Real</u> by Toni Raiten-D'Antonio.

My copy of the Velveteen Rabbit is worn from passing it around through the years. I wish I had been as creative as D'Antonio in revealing the hidden wisdom as appropriate today, as when the *Velveteen Rabbit* was written by Margery Williams in 1922.

I would have loved to have authored Toni Raiten-D'Antonio's book <u>*The Velveteen Principles – A Guide to Becoming Real*</u> *(1975)* based on the hidden wisdom of the children's book <u>Velveteen Rabbit,</u> Margery Williams (1922.

I endorse some of the ideas D'Antonio delineates on the objectifying of human beings by parents, the culture, and lastly by ourselves. Her main premise is the abandoning of our real selves to fit in and in the process we've become anxious, depressed, obsessed, compulsive, and lack empathy for ourselves and others. I beg clients to shelve the case against themselves and help them work through punitive standards no one could measure up to. We ask for perfection and the failure to be so leads to shame due to feelings of inadequacy.

"Stuff" has replaced a formerly bad definition of happiness and success. The price of becoming less than human is subtle in ads, peer groups, and entertainment fields. The pain and grief arise as the losses mount over grief, which leads to unhappiness, malaise, and other unwanted negative feelings. The unreal maintain crowded lives so there is no time to feel. The hidden purpose is to blot out feelings and produce distraction.

I'm in the middle of writing this section and I've stopped. I'm not sure what prompted my pulling out my old Oliver Perry Morton high school yearbook, (1959) Top Hat, Hammond, Indiana. I reread the "swell messages" my friends inscribed. "Swell" – last thing I wanted to be thought of. I'd long forgotten any of the autographs or even who the authors were. What really got my attention was one of the ads showing a Pepsi bottle cap. Only if you were a collector would you note the single dot as opposed to the double dot. I pulled out of my marriage the memory of all the collected Pepsi memorabilia and managed to color the yearbook ad. We truly care for our past, present and future. Thank goodness I have let go of the sadness and have only the nostalgia of all the trips collecting bottles, ads, and signage.

What do you ask has that to do with objectifying? I never paid any attention to old ads or collectibles. It became my entire life and not because I was enraptured. It started as perfectimistic to please my husband. It was where I could receive attention, conversation, and go on antique trips. I'm not saying there was no fun, but rather a subtle surrendering of self that I just now became aware of.

When you are ready to venture back out into the relationship world, pick up some material reviews to aid your recovery. Two books I find simple, comprehensive, and relevant are Dating for Dummies and the Everything Dating Book.

In Joy Browne's Dating for Dummies, the radio talk host tackles every conceivable way to be an expert date. The only thing left would be a slide out partner on a CD. The Everything Dating Book is mostly featuring info to become "a smart, savvy, effective, and satisfied single, and to date well and happily until you find your match.

PART III – THRIVING

THRIVING

INTRODUCTION

This part introduces ways for you to take back self-control and begin to live fully. As I've said, I found myself "other-focused" most of my life, trying to serve and please. Perhaps, it was a cultural position. It afforded me great benefits, such as economic security (at least the fantasy of it), excluded being alone, afforded some social respect, and protection.

In order to thrive I was going to have to make room for my new life. My inner space was cluttered with old photos, resentments, and stale memories. I was tired of replaying the story, talking about it, and re-experiencing the pain. It was time to honor: I had reclaimed my disowned pieces. I was ready to reactivate my joyful self, but at the price of a loss of a sense of self.

What if you find yourself wallowing in the quagmire of a three year old or more terminated relationship? Read the Velveteen Rabbit and the Velveteen Principles. See if you can identify with these twelve principles:

1. Real is Possible
2. Real is a Process
3. Real is Emotional
4. Real is Empathetic
5. Real is Courageous
6. Real is Honest
7. Real is Generous
8. Real is Grateful
9. Real can be Painful
10. Real is Flexible
11. Real love Endures
12. Real is Ethical (Velveteen Principles vii and viii)

Have you taken the time to tell your story and complete the assessments in Section 1? Have you been writing in your journal? What about the thought provoking self-reflection exercises at the end of each chapter of Striving? Seek professional help if you are unable to use self-help materials. We are looking at small increments of change over time.

Note your certificate of completion and a place for you to check your own grade depending on effort and understanding. Ask for help—the number one coping strategy underutilized by most of us.

This section is about thriving in spite of all of our losses. The complexity of our human personality and spirit allow us to have many emotions and thoughts coexisting at the same time.

We may go with the flow, slow the process, or even jump to another place. It is about your journey and not arriving at a particular destination by someone else's watch.

Now that we've survived and begun a new self-directed pathway, it is time to honor our new more positive self-assessment…..Thriving. If you don't recognize your forward movement, you will probably stop moving forward. Your internal feedback loop needs to instruct your brain you are in a more positive healing mode.

CHAPTER 9
A KALEIDOSCOPIC VIEW

I'm holding my kaleidoscope reflecting on the little girl who dreamed of escaping a most dysfunctional environment. The pieces of glass remained constant through the years, trapped between the prisms. I am aware of how I have avoided painful situations by withdrawing to protect myself to manage my fears. Sometimes, not having a partner would send out a distress signal with a resulting sadness. My obsessive-compulsive sets manifested by education across three domains reflected how I was able to intellectualize and keep my life in a neat bundle, moving forward in the achievement domain.

Following the divorce, I turned to all my text books, self-help materials, and copiously writing notes for Palm Island. Even after all this, I was never going to live my dream—only write about it as a loss. I was content to maintain a low personal profile in favor of a high professional practice.

I slowly began to heal from the inside out. There was no quantum leap. It has been a self-directed journey. The pieces of colored glass in the kaleidoscope can represent all my potentiality and possible pathways. My desire to fuse with a mate will probably never disappear. I am more forgiving of myself and others for making mistakes and not always being able to redirect my attachment hunger. As I review these last few years, I am more fully aware of how far reaching my early childhood was on not accepting my husband's desire to be divorced. It was not at all an act of withholding, but rather of self-preservation. I couldn't bare the thought of losing him.

I grew up in a culture that valued thoughts over feelings. Essentially, though, thought without feeling results in a colorless existence. In reverse, feeling without thought can result in impulsive acting out. A marriage of both feeling and thought can result in a meaningful existence that is emotionally satisfying. Our expectations and beliefs are amendable. To accurately tune into our inner worlds, we need an understanding of both our emotional and cognitive status.

Probably most significant for me is how I experience myself now: a spirit/soul inhabiting an aging body. My spirit/soul vies for time and attention and that spiritual personality is often at the mercy of the rest of life's demands. Talking about my traumatic experiences has aided my recovery, as has the enormous amount of writing and compiling I have completed over the past four years.

Pilgrim's Progress

My outer world crumbled as my inner world grew. In actuality, I was growing in wisdom and understanding within the abyss.

Emotional literacy means putting your feelings into words and keeping your inner world well versed on where you are and formulating new goals. No inner world? It is never too late to develop—or maybe a better term is, access--yours.

Within you, your shadow side—where destructive emotions lie—contains hostility and anger. By bringing these thoughts and feelings into consciousness, we are able to integrate negative aspects of ourselves and work through them. Creativity is said to inhabit the shadow. One aspect is the desire to isolate and punish ourselves. This desire stems from an avoidance of failure, so we prohibit any social demands on our person that looks like taking more risk and possible failure.

Reactions from the Breakup

Your self can experience healthy humility-- recognize self-imperfection that exists in all human beings. Remember, our emotions have goals. We feel fearful and want safety. Rage is always about the past and is self-defeating. Anger acts as a stand-in for working through our losses and setting new goals. Anger can also provide information, so that we need to control our confrontations. Intense anger is not trustworthy. Ancient anger—anger we have harbored from past hurts—is loaded with resentments and frustrations. Stress can produce emotional upsets and changes of mood. The loneliness resulting from the breakup is most dreaded and leaves us restless and feeling rejected. Our belief systems and fellowship with God can help us overcome the loneliness. Later, we tiptoe out again and find the courage to invest in new relationships.

Your self has a philosophical system it has lived by. I wasn't brought up to minimize my losses. There was no prescription to work through and heal oneself. You lived with whatever happened to you and were expected to survive it with courage. Failure to do so can result in our living in the past in our heads, despite going through the motions of present living. We also create fear and anxiety for the future for having too little control. Living with loss is not akin to working through the loss and growing a self that can live fully in spite of the loss.

Divorce consumes energy and leaves us anxious and weary. My spiritual self can also hurt, feel exhausted, and want to pull in to heal. In our desperate hours, we long for a different family of origin, history, or more promising economic conditions. In essence, our spiritual development involves struggles for us to grow. As with my shadow side, sometimes I failed to seek comfort in communion with God. Turning to others for core needs only a relationship with the Divine can fill when my attachment hunger reared its ugly head. Inspirational readings, going to the Word, and fellowship with friends paled compared to becoming everything for a partner. Others cannot heal our early childhood wounds. A spiritual journey yielded the results I needed to become whole for the first time.

Even in my depleted times, I can organize a workshop on a spiritual topic and rev up my existential energy. Our tendency towards isolation is very strong, but self-knowledge, determination, and a strong commitment to growth replenish us faster than withdrawal. I thought my creative self had to be engaged. It was not as prophetic as in happier times. I was actually programming myself to shut off and down.

Your Shadow Self

Carl Jung referred to a complex of undeveloped feelings, ideas, and desires as the negative side of the ego. Your shadow self is my shadow side found herself cloaked in shame and fear of failure, coupled with distrust. She was bound by the tethers of expectations, and she found out that "rocky road" not only referred to the flavor of the month but a bitter pathway of sorrow. She was forced to reign in her bitterness and reach for betterness and gratefulness.

I designed some exercises for my shadow self. Perhaps they will give you some ideas for your own "Shadow Talk."

Lighting Up Your Shadows

Have a heart-to-heart conversation with that part of you wish you could disown—for example, your fearful, ashamed, scared-child side. Close your eyes and imagine one of the hurts you have recently experienced. See the person who wounded you sitting across the room. Write down everything you would like to say to that person, knowing there will be no repercussions. Be very specific as to:

> what the hurt is
>
> how it has influenced you
>
> what changes have occurred due to this wound.

Now, look at what you wrote down and identify the various sub-personalities that prompted them. For example,

> the jealous one
>
> the angry one
>
> the vengeful one.

Next, call on your spiritual self:

What would the dialogue look like between the wounded and the spiritual self? Let these two parts of you talk to each other. What are you finding out? What is the spiritual self saying? Is it helpful? Write down the conversation you overhear.

Remember, the person who hurt you cannot fix you. Only your intention to forgive and actually letting go of the pain will help you heal. If all your resentment and anger really helped, you'd be over the hurt by now.

Remember something else: you don't have to overcome all your conflicts and inhibitions or concern yourself with minor fears of abandonment or engulfment. These are only a nuisance and will disappear over time.

Remember what I shared with you .....how I imagine myself approaching God's throne. I spill all my pain and suffering, begging for mercy and a quick fix. Instead, he reminds me of the four pots with double chickens that I ignore for the one empty one. This helps keep me centered and humble. Construct your own dialogue to help you accept losses.

Important Realizations

I've offered my personal story because it is almost unbelievable to recognize the stranglehold an addictive relationship has had on your emotional self.

This self—yourself—can now own the anger of not being able to totally control your significant other and know this aspect of yourself is feeding on negative fear, rage, jealousy, and hostility. Almost everything negative falls under the umbrella of fear. A depressed self-concept is at a higher risk for fears and anxious feelings.

The villain you have now to fear is not your ex-partner but yourself. We are all complex and imperfect; and at some point forgiveness will be the pathway of inner peace and being in sync with ourselves. Core hits—such as you've experienced—leave deep scars that temporarily make one experience a loss of a sense of self. Many relationships suffer years of physical and/or emotional abuse. However, this book has focused on high-functioning marriages, in which the partners shared, communicated at least some, and enjoyed each other. And then, in which one partner through betrayal, withdraws emotionally, and eventually physically.

Healthy relationships are based on equality, mutuality, and reciprocity. Engel's (2000) *Loving Him (or Her) Without Losing You* makes the crucial point that we must stop disappearing and start being ourselves if a relationship can really work.

An addictive relationship is marginal at best. The couple are co-conspirators who silently contract to not discuss a mirage of issues, and both become conflict avoidant. Lack of problem solving deteriorates intimacy over time, and one or both are unaware of the disintegration of the coupleship. A marginal relationship that one or both leave may prompt inner work for a stronger possibility of a healthy partnership in the future.

It takes two selves who are authentic to not lose themselves in the relationship. Spending too much time trying to heal a sick spouse wears out intimacy. When a relationship works, underneath all the public masks and facades exist two authentic individuals who need to have healed from past relationships through deep inner reflection. Self-discovery takes time and effort. Only when you are intimate with yourself can you be intimate with another.

Engel (2000) in *Loving Him (or Her) Without Losing You* addresses solitude, facing fears of loneliness, reconnecting with nature, listening to one's inner voice about our feelings, and reclaiming our disowned emotions.

Engel's advice is to become a person of substance who is no longer imprisoned inside a self overly dependent on one other person. She sees the self as longing to know itself and be connected socially and with the natural environment. Our feelings become disowned in childhood and disappear entirely out of conscious awareness. We couple to gain wealth and fame through the other. She advocates an equal intimate, loving relationship not obtained by giving up a sense of self.

Solitude has assumed a bad rap in our society and is not embraced by my clients.

Loneliness is often an artificial state created by never being comfortable with aloneness. Engel suggests by knowing ourselves, honoring our feelings, and developing a strong inner life our needs are better met by ourselves. We can communicate more accurately to others and avoid projecting our own thoughts and feelings on partners.

Stressed, frustrated, hurt, abandoned, or betrayed, coming through the healing, I now put my emphasis on trusting myself to survive and eventually thrive in spite of life's losses. In the past, my fears directed my behavior, which set me up for such disappointment. Losses are inevitable, frustrations tolerable, and all stress unavoidable. My history is mine. My suffering—a badge I completed and grew from.

Now, more and more, I accept others, see them make mistakes, and in general realize they are not targeting me. Rather, they are doing what works for them.

The SELF Model, Revisited

Remember the SELF model: Surviving, Examining, Letting go, and Fashioning. This is a management model, not some type of cure, and it requires dedication and work. Many processing words operate on a continuum, having positive and negative sides that for me require a middle of the road normal position. Too much or too little of most of these actions puts me out of touch with being healthy. For example: For me:

Surviving – All I can do in the beginning.

However, to remain in this condition is to surrender life. It is a constriction of my environment, over-guarded and less willing to take risks. It represents an unhealed position, perhaps fearful. The sadness and depression within this model are also appropriate feelings to inform me of needing to make change. Happiness during a loss would represent avoidance and not be real. Our feelings signal us that something is wrong. Our problem-solving skills help us right the wrong.

Examining – If I over-examine and am too analytical I miss living my life spontaneously and in a lighthearted fashion. With no examining I am living unaware of who I am and where I am. Scared and anxious remind me I need to take care of myself financially and monitor addictive tendencies. Growth may bring on fear of changing. Knowing myself through self-reflection and feedback mechanisms is a positive way to change.

Letting-Go – I am me. I need to let-go of what isn't working and not erase all that I am. My negative events shaped my life as my positive ones. I do need to let go of negative feelings that have risen from negative events by working through my losses.

Marvin was my friend. He and my other landlords Gene and Ivan offered support as my marriage disintegrated. Marvin's death fused with my painful state as I mourned the sudden loss of a friend and my partner.

Fashioning – I am my history, present, and future. My core self has known me and is secure in both the positive and negative events that shaped my life. I decide what needs to remain constant and what needs modification. I am a work in progress.

Too glad might represent denial and lack of empathy for others. Joyful and living fully in the here and now is a healthy place to strive for.

Spend a couple of moments looking at the loss model. You see the four quadrants:

Surviving

Examining

Letting-Go

Fashioning

- We move back and forth throughout our life cycle with small and large losses.

The most inner circle represents me and the thoughts and feelings that are mine alone. Traumatic experiences (death, divorce, threats, etc.) render us out of control. Beginning with the word containing and going clock wise the letters spell out controls. The eight processes containing, obtaining, negating, taking-in,

129

reflecting, offsetting, laughing, and spiriting are not the only actions we engage in. These represent my personal model for replacing my hopelessness, helplessness, and haplessness with empowerment. In essence, I am most reactive during the survival period and can minimally interact with the environment to contain and obtain what I want and need. My heart is heavy (sad and depressed) and dampens my motivation to be creative. It is an emotionally flooding place. When I can examine from a more cognitive advantage, I am able to negate some of my negative feelings and continue to contain myself. I know how complex I am and can have competing thoughts and feelings while processing any or the entire model. My anxiety needs to be managed while I sort through all my losses. I can harness some of the energy to regain control by taking in new information and support. Anger shuts off my ability to grieve and engage in a letting-go process. Off-setting with respite activities, new goals will distract me temporarily and renew my spirit to continue the processing of my feelings and thoughts.

I'm now operating in a more controlled place, navigating in a more spiritual and fun-loving way in spite of the trauma. I learn I can be sad at times and still reinvest in pleasurable pursuits. Over-controlled or under-controlled affords little peace. Only when I reside in the middle of the continuum am I able to both attend and concentrate.

The Four Modes: Surviving, Examining, Letting-Go, Fashioning

When we are in a survivor mode, our sadness and depression has been activated by the environment or some condition within our bodies. We have needs that trigger an obtaining process. We also must contain whatever is operating internally or externally.

For example: A dissolution of a marriage. We would experience sadness and depression. We would need to obtain emotional support, perhaps financial advice, legal assistance, and other resources. Our containment would be to emotionally pull ourselves together to continue our daily tasks and mentally manage our losses. Examining ourselves after the divorce would provide corrective information as well as inform us of our losses. We might choose to negate future worries and deal with them later, or we might make plans to include prevention of future situation, for example, if you know financially keeping the family home will be a future burden to maintain it; you might choose to sell and move quickly to another more supportive environment. Letting-go of the marriage would include self-reflection of what roles I played and corrective action for new relationships. Only by owning my own mistakes can I hope to grow. Off-setting might include returning to school to help deal with the time I now have on my hands because I've relocated to a smaller place. Fashioning anew, we would involve embracing fun and rejoicing again at my special gifts, blessings, and callings. I can visualize my own color wheel where..........

- The outer red ring symbolizes feelings and feeling states (overuse of a feeling).

- The inner yellow ring is a color wheel with various processing operations representing actions.

- At my best, I prefer being in "Fashioning", full of gladness, and launching in a spiritual direction. I would guess this might be your goal too.

- Accepting that life is not stagnant, my wheels rotate both the outer red ring and the inner yellow color wheel. My job is to use good self-talk and problem solving to seek shelter and act when necessary. Doing my job enables I to examine what has happened, let go, and move back into glad-fashioning.

  Even good change involves loss of the familiar. I may find myself angry and frustrated at changing, and the challenge of growth.

As you can see, and no doubt have experienced, loss does not wrap up into a neat little package. We move back and forth among the "circles" and can be challenged in any phase by any process with multiple moods and feelings. Our real work is to problem solve and move gently and gradually, or sometimes harshly and quickly, into fashioning. This is where I prefer to reside—home base, so to speak—glad, adventurous, forgiving, looking forward.

Self-CONTROLS

In reviewing the SELF-process, I've identified some very helpful self-controls. You could make your own list. They have been tools for keeping me on course, and I'm glad to share them with you in a more specific manner:

1. C ontaining
2. O btaining
3. N egating
4. T aking in
5. R eflecting
6. O ffsetting
7. L aunching
8. S piriting

I designed these as part of my self-healing and journaled about them. Here I offer you a distillation of my notes. Use them as you need to.

Containing

Let me construct doors behind which I can place various events, problems, or past situations. This way I can remain better in control, moving in and out when I prefer to. But watch out—too much containment, and I lose my spontaneity; too little and I'm chaotic.

Obtaining

I need to be self-sufficient economically. It helps me feel safe to be in control of credit, spending, and other needs by identifying them and understanding "norms". This is how I feel safe. But also, I realize that being content with what I have and not always obtaining serves my sense of self-actualizing. I need to share to grow.

Negating

I need to control, minimizing what events have meant to me on a personal level. By understanding and forgiving, I can honestly move forward. Otherwise, I will serve up rage, so hidden from my conscious self, simmering and awaiting an uncorking. I need to negate the negative talk. However, I don't want to do this before I hear the messages, so I know what I'm thinking and feeling and fear. It is a balance that begs attention.

Taking in

I want to take in advice, information, and avoid addictions. By choosing what, when, and how much to take in, I am exercising choices. Overuse can lead to abuse. Blame requires self-monitoring and program adjustments.

Reflecting

With too much reflection, I live in yesterdays. With too little, I've lost who I am and where I've come from. And I ignore or throw away well-earned lessons. All my losses have processed and permitted a joyful, glad, heart to reign. Only by self-reflection and acceptance can I move on from the event and not remain of it, stuck and replaying it.

Offsetting

Goals have been sometimes thwarted. I run my psychic accounting and remember all I have; to offset the have-nots of my life. Surrender is not about me, but about goals that no longer serve me. I maintain a healthy tab.

Might there be room for gratitude here?

Launching

This is an ongoing process of using all my gifts, resisting stagnation and a well-concealed lazy streak. However, taking on too much at one time can shut everything down for a short while. Balance and harmony are more attitudinal than reality-based. It is how I think and feel at the present moment for each day I grow and change. My desire is to do so without fanfare in a natural progression and once in a while welcome a quantum leap from the experience.

Spiriting

I use this word for adding action to my spiritual self. Meditation, Christian music, and fellowship do not just happen. They are planned—taken off the top. I have incorporated these into my exercise program; spiritual exercise is as important as physical.

But guilt can interfere with enjoyment if your perfectionist self is in charge. If you feel you've crossed your spiritual value system, it will take the steps of forgiveness to lessen the strangle hold of guilt. Perfectionism is self-righteous and ignores our humanness.

I hope you've used the three Appendix sets to construct your journal/scrapbook. Keep this in mind as you go through your own journey. Use the tools here, fashion your own, and you will come through what you need to. And thank you for being a part of Palm Island.

CHAPTER 10
EPILOGUE

A full circle . . . as in Part I, for comfort I quoted from "Resurrection" by L.C.M., now here I celebrate with more lines:

My soul soars:

    I feel personally involved with others.

    I stand alone now, yet am unafraid.

    No hand is held in mine;

    I stand alone, independent…alive.

Viewing the dawn,

    I feel the blood surge through my body,

    and laugh, grateful for the rebirth of my

    spirit.

But through the brightness of the dawn,

    Memories still return.

There is a difference –

    They do not plague,

    but help to form the future.

Like the speaker here, I too have had to accept my aloneness and, at times, my loneliness. I have discovered many different wellsprings to replenish myself and fear less judgment and abandonment that were formerly so frightening.

I have witnessed a rekindling of my spirit. Footprints by Margaret Fishback Powers comes to mind. Not only her best loved poem, but a little inspirational book that is a beach walk with the Lord. I am encouraged to trust new dreams that will lead to many new places.

Finally, I am finishing the unfinished business of closing Palm Island. My book almost completed is representative of a fantasy never to be lived out in reality. Four times hurricanes on the East or West Coast have prohibited my trip. I both dread and am anxious to make this final pilgrimage to say goodbye.....to my Palm Island lot, surrendered in divorce to Palm Island itself.

Palm Island represents, and represented for me, a strong sense of community— unique and united by ownership. Everyone waves; everyone says hello as I navigate my rented "golf cart." There is a sense of belonging missing from my urban centered life. It is a wave of recognition you are welcome here. It has plagued me that I must surrender this world. I returned to Palm Island to say goodbye. I chose a candle lighting ceremony because of the spiritual space it creates for letting go of the past.

I light a candle on the dock and say goodbye to the lot I—we—cherished so much and a future lifestyle never to be. There is just one more closure. . . Palm Island itself.

I spent three days at the Palm Island Resort, Unit 2011, made to order. My rental is on the Gulf, artfully detailed, regal colors, warm and inviting, and so practically accommodating in every way. My stay included great food at the restaurant, super service, and the beach.

My heart was happy and purring in this blissful space. It was love at first sight and such a fit! I recalled Isaiah 61:1-3:

> The Lord has anointed me to comfort
>
> all who mourn, and to bestow on them
>
> a crown of beauty instead of ashes,
>
> the oil of gladness, instead of mourning
>
> and a garment of praise instead of despair.

It now holds a special personal meaning. It was 5:00 a.m. in the morning when I had my final epiphany. Sitting on the beach, I had just watched a shooting star flash across the heavens. And I realized that now I was in another place emotionally. Sifting sand between my fingertips, I was sorting out my ambivalence about this final farewell. Oh, how much I have missed being here! My eyes were misty from being so moved by my emotions and past memories.

And then I came to the hardest part … telling my island I wouldn't be back. I know now it was my fantasy that my husband and I would live and work here. It could never have been his dream. More accurately, it was probably his nightmare. He had pulled his love out long before. He hated the sun, never beached, was bored with shelling, and never initiated anything remotely island, except with our friends. The experience was totally intellectualized. Palm Island for him was financial prospects and little more at that time.

He had climbed out of my dream long before the divorce. We had never had a hand-in-hand. The fantasy was all of my own creation. It was always my Palm Island; my dream of retiring here.

There will be more losses, more mistakes, roads not taken out of fear, missed signposts, and a sea of possible regrets. My attachment hunger is alive and well, but I'm more aware of its desires. And my flights of fantasy still take off, but I've created a new landing strip to keep a better handle on them. There will also be new adventures, multiple callings, and Palm Island once more.

My shadow has its pictures in my photo album. I know all about this negative side and have placed a "heart monitor" on it. I will never understand all my selves, but will seek my spiritual self to align with the value system I embrace. I have asked God for forgiveness for my shortcomings. I strive to live fully, respecting where I've come from and how I can change my self-talk.

Palm Island.....

I love you. I don't need ownership. I need you! I never will say goodbye to you. Only...until the next time we meet. I want to experience the aliveness and feeling of safety surrounded by your majesty. I've sifted sand and scoured the beaches to share a handful of sand dollars with my clients. No one owns this beauty...the legacy is for all of us. I will continue to walk your beaches and heal my spirit/soul.

No, there will be no closure for Palm Island Resort and Unit 2011. I have made reservations for Mother's Day. I am planning annual pilgrimages and inviting mothers who have lost their sons and daughters to this healing place. It will be a special spiritual retreat.

It isn't only how I feel about Palm Island that beckons me here, but how I feel about myself. I am grateful for all my blessings and those who love me as I am. I want my life to be purposeful. I want you to seek your spiritual self and recognize that God has given you the gifts to change pathways and embrace other callings.

I wait at the Crossroads cheering you on, reminding you to renew yourself. All our changes start with intentions. A life well lived is an art form, our purpose and our duty. God does not stop to cull out the qualified. He qualifies those He calls!

I wish you success, courage, and love on your journey. As I have fashioned my life again, so can you. You are not alone.

PART IV:

APPENDIXES

APPENDIX A:

ASSESSMENTS

Use these assessments in any order to help yourself corral and take hold of your emotions, detach from them, and go forward with next actions.

Your Story

These exercises will help you focus on where you are now.

1. Write your own story of betrayal.
2. What were your initial reactions?
3. Who was there for you?
4. If you are still experiencing sadness and painful times, write down what appears to trigger these times.
5. If you have children, how are you dealing with joint parenting?

Parenting books that could be helpful:

Touchpoints 1992

    T.B. Brazelton, M.D.

    Perseus Books, Reading, MA

    (Pregnancy through 3 years plus Challenges to Development.)

Why Can't We Talk?

    Mil. Trujillo

    (What Teens would share if Parents would Listen. Health Communications, Inc., Deerfield Beach, FL

Your Survival Statements

1. I need…..

    A safe place to live.

    Family and friends to love me.

    To pull in from other pursuits as much as possible.

    Plenty of rest and mild exercise.

    Continue this list with what else you need.

2. I need not to…..

    Make major decisions until I'm more together.

    Strike out at the person who hurt me.

    Turn to addictions.

    Continue this list with what else you need not do, be, or have.

3. Analyze what happened…..

    It isn't what happened as much as how it has, is, and will affect my life.

4. As I begin to accept my situation I can…..

    Analyze what happened and my personal significance

    Take responsibility for myself.

    Form a plan to heal myself.

    Continue this list with what else you can do.

Surviving:

Here are exercises to help you through each of the aspects of the SELF model. Use these exercises in conjunction with the chapters.

1. Take the time to list all the hurtful things that were said to you. Cross off any with no truth. Now star those things you need to work on <u>because you have chosen to.</u>

2. Make a list of all the horrible things you said. Now, cross out anything that was untrue. Star those things you put up with. How do they compare with Number 1? If you cannot accomplish this now, come back later when you can.

3. Now, list those qualities you like about yourself. Remember, no matter what was said, it only represents a part of the truth at best.

4. Close your eyes and tell yourself you are hurting now, and loved still by family and friends. Name each one and feel their love: _____. Most of all turn to God for the strength to take this solitary journey that has been forced upon you. Tell yourself you can do it.

5. Travel inside your head—use your imagination—to a safe place (a lake, a mountain cabin, a summer camp, an island). Remind yourself of all the peace and serenity you feel there. Breathe slowly.

Examining

1. In time, an active me would like to…
   - Be assertive: speak up for truth
   - Make conscious decisions
   - Share with friends
   - Identify angry thoughts and control acting on them
   - Work through painful memories.
   - Continue this list with other things and activity you would like to do.
   - Place your marriage under a microscope.
   - Look at the mix: If the red jellybeans represent your mate and the green ones are you, answer the following:
     a) Are some of the beans separate so that each of you has an identity apart from the relationship?
     b) Are there some beans mixed?
     c) Was the marriage interactive?
     d) Was it equal in power and responsibility?
     e) What sentiments were present on each side?
     f) Was it overall a good enough fit?
     g) Do you tell yourself you wasted X number of years? Revisit this position and list the positive aspects as well as the negative ones.
     h) What do you wish you had done differently?
     i) What do you wish your partner had done differently?

j) Have you picked other partners like this one or been chosen by the same type of partner?

k) On a 0-10 scale, try to honestly represent how

_____the relationship met your needs and wants.

_____met his needs and wants.

_____have furthered individual growth as persons.

Letting Go: Self-Reflection

1. List the losses you have experienced prior to your separation or divorce. Give approximate dates.

2. Have you worked through all of them or are they still negatively impacting your life? (If there is still residue, take heart--this loss will pick it up!)

3. Now list the losses that are present or yet to come as a result of this traumatic event. Place a checkmark by the ones you know you can handle.

Possible Losses from Breakup:

   i.   Family residence
   ii. Mutual friendships
   iii. Lifestyle
   iv. Economic position
   v.   Full time with children
   vi. Relatives that will now be distanced
   vii. Respect from family, friends, and institutions
   viii. job

1. Write a letter to yourself as if a friend was authoring it. How would your friends encourage you? What would they point out as your personality traits to help you face this list and heal? Be generous to yourself.

2. One way to finish unfinished business--leftover hurts, for example--is to recall the events that contributed to the bad feelings. Choose one event from Question 1. What messages are you still giving yourself to reinforce the pain? Change the message! Let go of the ancient hurt. Remind yourself how long you've been renting space to this event and the pain.

3. Soothe yourself by giving yourself new messages concerning your ability to now deal with it. Forgive the person who wronged you. Review the section on forgiveness, if you need to. That doesn't mean putting yourself back in that vulnerable place but becoming larger, more expansive. See yourself as more than a hurt victim. See yourself as able to forgive and radiate love instead.

Remember the movie "Under the Tuscan Sun?" (If not, rent it!) It is a romantic comedy where a young woman seeks a new life following her husband's infidelity. In the pursuit of her passion to refurbish an old villa, she rediscovers herself.

Letting Go: Self-Exploration

Here are some statements to help you and prompt you to more accurate self-exploration. Fill in the blanks to evaluate where you are right now.

1. I_____ (have/do not have) control issues. I am _____ (over-controlled, under-controlled).
2. I feel I need to be_____(more, less) controlled because_____ _____
3. After rereading my story, I feel _____
4. My partner_____(had/did not have) grandiose expectations and insatiable cravings that I could not fulfill.
5. I would _____ (miss/not miss) my mate if I _____ (had material support independent of the relationship/could find someone else).
6. If I were really honest with myself, the marriage was _____ (terrible for both of us/terrible for him/terrible for me/good for him/good for me).
7. I_____ (feel/do not feel) diminished for suffering the betrayal.
8. When I try to think about the relationship and what happened I _____ (am/ am not) overwhelmed.
9. There are many ways I could stop myself from hurting and ruminating over events. I can list three:
    a. _____
    b. _____
    c. _____

10. What other losses have you experienced as an individual or a couple that might have some bearing on the "situation"? List them. The loss of a child is devastating to any marriage. Economic woes, illness, and loss of friends also impact relationships.

11. I _____ (look/do not look) back over the course of the relationship and identify problems that I avoided talking about.

12. What can you say to yourself about present circumstances and how you can heal yourself?

13. Change one sentence in your self-talk by not beating up on yourself.
Example: I am too fat.

Self-talk change: I am not content with my weight and need to make a plan to change, exercise, diet, or join a group.

I can use self-talk:

14. What if I do run into my ex-partner? I do not have to say or do anything. I can trust myself to deal appropriately. I may choose not to frequent places where the likelihood would be great.

Fashioning: Identifying Strengths and Weaknesses

This is a quick way to know where you think and feel you are.

Take a minute and form two columns: one your strengths and the other your weaknesses—or should we say "challenges"?

Some practical considerations such as engaging in an exercise program to increase energy might move a weakness out of the "weakness" column.

Now, create another column on how the relationship fared in supporting your individual growth.

My Example: (Make your own heading)
Individual Growth: (Make notes)

Social Aspects	Financial Aspects	Intellectual Aspects	Cultural Aspects
Increased Friendships	Worked together &	Finished College	Saw 4 Broadway
Learned to dance	built a company		plays
Played Tennis			

Identification of My Strengths and Weaknesses

APPENDIX B:

EXERCISES

Creative Corner

If you've been resistant to participate, I still invite you to.....

Write your own story, first your prologue and later your epilogue

Complete the assessment tools in Appendix A.

Begin a notebook, journal, or scrapbook to house your thoughts, feelings, and healings.

Use the self-help materials referred to in this book as well as creating your own.

Activities

Choose one or more of these activities per week. Add your own as they come to you.

1. Light a candle in remembrance of all that your relationship contained. Respect yourself and your partner who has moved on by honoring what was significant and not to be forgotten. Keep this exercise simple and meaningful. Losses need recognition. They can neither be avoided or undone.

2. Use music to soothe and relax yourself in the bath, the car, and the kitchen and while you walk.

3. Use tapes or CDs that contain affirmations of healing, such as those by Wayne Dyer and Louise Hay. Many bookstores have sections for these. These tapes can be great played as you fall asleep.

4. Put candles, music, and bubble bath in the bathroom for a relaxation time.

5. Choose walks over food or alcohol. If you have a gym membership, force yourself to go. You know by now that exercise helps relieve stress and release positive brain chemicals.

6. Use respite – a break from the pain – by having lunch or coffee with a friend. Talk about something else.

7. Use small slips of paper to identify your losses. Put them in a box and only take them out one at a time for mourning instead of listing and dealing with everything at once.

8. Write a letter to yourself reminding yourself of other times you were able to overcome a traumatic event or loss. Encourage yourself to accept the sadness and pain and know they will weaken in time with your help.

9. Use an affirmation – some combination of positive words to help you get through your day. You may pick scriptures out of the Old Testament or New Testament. A daily prayer book might be helpful.

10. Create a safe place indoors or outdoors or at a park where you can light a candle and seek comfort from God to help you work through your suffering.

11. Stop by your faith-based place for comfort during the week.

APPENDIX C:

MY MAXIMS

Attitude Adjustment

For a While They
Covered my Walls. Now
The Best Helped Mend
My Heart.....

Attitude

By

Charles Swindoll

"The longer I live, the more I realize the impact of attitude on life. Attitude, to me, is more important than facts. It is more important than the past, than education, than money, than circumstances, than failures, than successes, than what other people think or say or do. It is more important than appearance, giftedness or skill. It will make or break a company...a church...a home.

The remarkable thing is we have a choice every day regarding the attitude we will embrace for that day. We cannot change our past...we cannot change the fact that people will act in a certain way. We cannot change the inevitable. The only thing we can do is play on the one string we have, and that is our attitude...I am convinced that life is 10% what happens to me and 90% how I react to it.

And so it is with you...we are in charge of our Attitudes". Remember this. Nothing more needs to be said.

Pilgrim Post-Its

As co-travelers exploring the traumatic events associated with relationship losses, I have identified what I call little Pilgrim Post-its that remind me of various stops along the way. These are simply "stickies" on which I write favorite and meaningful sayings and passages that help remind me, bolster me, and keep me going. I have found it helpful to keep various ones at my desk and computer to mark my progress as well as to guide my steps. Of course, you can plaster them anywhere you wish, where you'll see them often. Here are some of mine. Perhaps you would like to make up your own.

1. The longest journey in the world begins with the first step.
2. If I ever go looking for my heart's desire again, I won't look any further than my own backyard, because if it isn't there, I never really lost it. (Dorothy in *The Wizard of Oz*)
3. Be a model—sometimes that is all you can do.
4. I think I can, I think I can, I can...I can...I can. (*The Little Engine That Could*)
5. But..., sometimes I cannot do it! (This author)
6. Wisdom still leads the heart that believes. (Best Christmas card 2005 – Day Spring Collection.)
7. Death will find you in a closet. Life will never look.
8. Men are taught to apologize for their weaknesses, women for their strengths. The divorced are simply seen as rejected lovers.
9. Unfortunately, survivors have to maintain a constricted world in order to feel in control. Life participants work through losses and move on, expanding their worlds.
10. Defeat:
11. Sits in his chair staring at the gray doves on the porch. He holds his hand underneath his heart, fingers curled tightly into themselves, glued together in a paralyzed rage. He is unwilling to go forward and unable to let go. He

151

is not blind or deaf, but it is unclear what he hears. He had a stroke six years ago and sleeps most of the day. In response to questions he answered yes or no interchangeably. Speech has lost all meaning. (Ruth Gendler, The *Book of Qualities*)

12. A list of names is not a support system.
    a. One has to actually perceive others as supportive to chart them as comforters.
13. My feelings are equal to your thinking. In control does not always mean at peace.
14. There are three forms of feedback to show disapproval:
    a. A complaint = very specific, a request for a change.
    b. Criticism = usually contains words such as "always" and "never" and is invariably unflattering.
    c. Contempt = refers to a person in global derogatory terms: "You are just like your mother".
15. It's okay to hurt.
16. Hurt tells us something is wrong and needs to be addressed.
17. Hurt is complex because past hurts can intensify our present hurt feelings and thoughts.
18. Sometimes we set ourselves up for hurt by recreating earlier parental scenes in choosing a partner.
19. We each contain a "joy candle" that may flicker in hurtful times but gives us hope we will experience joy again.
20. Hurt, heart, and help are integrated in our grief process.
21. By listening to our hurt with our heart and mind we can soothe ourselves, accepting what we cannot change.
22. New self-talk – sending healing messages to ourselves and living more consciously (instead of on an unconscious level) -- can aid our recovery.
23. Only food and beverages come canned and can be reconstituted in minutes. Human beings need time to exercise change for healing hurts.
24. Sometimes you have to just feel the pain and do what is right anyway.
25. All relationships are challenged in a society that is permissive.

26. Conscious love is harder to create and sustain than an unconscious marriage.

27. Time does not heal all wounds. Time gives us time to heal our wounds if we choose to use it.

28. Emotional bone yards are the reservoirs for unfinished business.

29. My truth is not the only truth and may appear to be a lie when placed next to my partner's truth.

30. The only kiss of death is me giving up on myself.

31. God can be my pilot, co-pilot, or spare tire. His presence and absence speak to both my inability to operate non-spiritually and feel whole again.

32. No abuse is as bad as the abuse I can inflict on myself by taking over responsibility for my losses. Many losses just occur with neither my permission nor involvement. Blaming myself keeps me from problem solving.

33. "If only" keeps me in the past, "someday" keeps me in the future. Neither helps me resolve my present situation. Both can be integrated into a self.

34. Remember the lessons of the past but let go of the pain. Create future memories (plans, goals, excitement, and hope) that are grounded in the here and now (roots and wings).

35. "The way of a fool seems right to him, but a wise man listens to advice". (Proverbs 12:15).

36. Forgiveness is the feeling of peace that emerges as you take your hurt less personally, take responsibility for how you feel, and become a hero instead of a victim in the story you tell. (D. Luskin, *Forgive for Good*. 2002*)*

37. Therapy: It is a perspective in which clients are invited into collaborative conversations. We seek to help people see possibilities, be accountable for what they do, and take actions that will help move them on into the kind of future they hope for. (B. Bertolino and B. O'Hanlon, *Even from a Broken Web*, 1998).

38. Empty...feel your way through the nothingness until at last you feel ready to fill. (R. Snyder, *Words of Wisdom for Women*, 1997)

39. The fundamental building blocks of self-esteem are your core beliefs: your basic assumptions about your value in the world. Core beliefs determine to what degree you see yourself as worthy, safe, competent, powerful, autonomous, and loved. They also establish your sense of belonging and a basic picture of how you are treated by others. (McKay and Fanning, *Self-Esteem.*)

40. While it is impossible to overstate the role of nurturing and reassurance in love, it is also true that love itself is demanding and sometimes exhausting. (Love as an addiction in *Challenge of the Heart.*)

41. The difference between addicts and love addicts: The combination of dependency and manipulativeness that is observed in heroin addicts lies behind the addict's exploitativeness. Unsure of his own identity, the addict sees other people as objects to serve his needs. But for the drug addict, using people is only a means to other ends; for the love addict, possessing people is the end. (*Challenge of the Heart*)

42. Hyper giving on one end negates the mutuality that makes for a committed healthy relationship.

43. Although you may feel like you will die from a broken heart, it is more likely you will fear living with one.

44. Self-fulfillment, previously in the background because of service to the family system, now must move to the foreground.

45. Aging and biology have less effect on the self than a negative attitude.

46. True neediness will surface like never before in this time of being the unchosen.

47. Seinfeld (1996) interprets over-investment in a love partner as a sign of inner emptiness because there is so little sense of self independent of this object (*Splitting Up*)

Spiritual Corner

A Message from My Spiritual Self

Appreciate and meditate

You are alive!

You have survived!

You will thrive!

Old Testament Inspiration, Ps 146:3

Don't put your confidence in powerful people; there is no help for you there. When their breathing stops, they return to the earth, and in a moment all their plans come to an end. But happy are those who have the God of Israel whose hope is in the Lord their God...The Lord lifts the burdens of those bent beneath their loads.

I Choose Self-Control

From Max Lucado, *In Grace for the Moment*

I am a spiritual being...after this body is dead, my spirit will soar. I refuse to let what will rot rule the external.

I choose self-control

I will be drunk only by joy

I will be impassioned by my faith

I will be influenced by God

I will be taught only by Christ (...and those who support his teachings.)

I choose self-control

New Testament Inspiration Phil. 4:4

Always be full of joy in the Lord. I say it again...rejoice...

Vs. 6 Tell God what you need and thank him for all he has done. If you do this, you will experience God's peace. His peace will guard your hearts and minds as you live in Christ Jesus.

Your Turn

Does your spiritual self have a voice?

What might you be hearing?

Give yourself time and space to be still—take a few breaths—and listen to your heartbeat. Then listen to your heart.

BIBLIOGRAPHY

Akhtar, S. (1990)
>Inner Torment
>Jason Aronson, Inc.
>North Vale, NJ

Anderson, N. (2003)
>Emotional Longevity
>Penguin Putnam, Inc.
>New York, NY

Beattie, M. (1990)
>The Language of Letting Go
>Hazelden
>USA

Browne, J. (2006)
>Dating for Dummies
>Wiley Publications, Inc.
>Hoboken, NJ

Collins, B. (1997)
>Emotional Unavailability
>Contemporary Books
>Chicago, IL

D'Antonio, T. (2004)
>Velveteen Principles: A Guide to Becoming Real
>Health Communications, Inc.
>Deerfield Beach, FL

Denham, S. (1998)
>Emotional Development in Young Children
>Guilford Publications, Inc.
>New York, NY

Dunham, A. (2006)
>The Everything Dating Book
>F & W Publications, Inc.
>Avon, MA

Engels, B. (2000)
>Loving Him (or Her) Without Losing You
>J. Wiley & Sons, Inc.
>New York, NY

Gendler, R. (1998)
>The Book of Qualities
>Harper Perennial
>New York, NY

Greenwald, R. (2003)
    <u>Find a Husband After 35</u>
    Ballantine Books
    New York, NY

Halpern, H. (1982)
    <u>How to Break Your Addiction to a Person</u>
    Bantam
    New York, NY

Kadell, J. (1992)
    <u>Manatee in The Florida Survival Handbook</u>
    Coastal Publications
    Sarasota, FL

Kavanaugh, J. (1991)
    <u>Mystic Fire: The Love Poetry of James Kavanaugh</u>
    Nash Publishers
    Highland Park, IL

Kraft, W. (2000)
    <u>Ways of the Desert</u>
    The Hawthorn Pastoral Press
    New York, NY

Kuster, E. (1996)
    <u>Exorcising Your Ex</u>
    Simon & Schosler
    New York, NY

Laquet, W. (1996)
    <u>Short-Term Couples Therapy</u>
    Brunner/Mazel
    New York, NY

Lewis, K. (2001)
    <u>With or Without a Man</u>
    Bull Publishing
    Annapolis, MD

Matsakis, A. (1996)
    <u>Aphrodite</u>
    New Harbinger Publications, Inc.
    Oakland, CA

Pam, A. & Pearson, J. (1998)
    <u>Splitting Up</u>
    Guilford Press
    New York, NY

Solomon, M. & Siegel,D (2003)
    <u>Healing Trauma</u>
    W.W. Norton & Co.
    New York, NY

Straus, J. (2006)
    <u>Unhooked Generation</u>
    Hyperion Publishing
    New York. NY

Subotnik, R. & Harris, G. (2005)
    <u>Surviving Infidelity</u>
    Adams Media
    Avon, MA

Van der Kolk, B. (1987)
    <u>Psychological Trauma</u>
    Am. Psychiatric Press
    Washington, DC

Weldwood, J. (1985)
    <u>Challenge of the Heart</u>
    Shambhala Publishing
    Boston, MA

Williams, M. (1975)
    <u>The Velveteen Rabbit</u>
    Avon Camelot Books
    New York, NY

Williamson, M.
    <u>Illuminated Prayer</u>

Zohar, D. & Marshall, I. (2000)
    <u>Spiritual Intelligence</u>
    Bloomsbury Publishing
    New York, NY

Dr. Tarr offers workshops on relationship losses. Check out her website: www.griefworksinc.com *or call* 305-666-3650 *for more information.*

Printed in the United States
54471LVS00004B/13-112

9 781425 947712